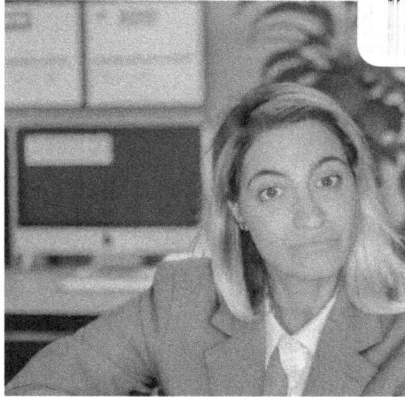

<u>Author of:</u>

1.) "Correcting Distortions of The Bible"
2.) "The Purpose of The Fall"

3.) "The Law of One- Condensed: Book 1"

4.) "The Law of One- Condensed: Book 2"
5.) "The Law of One- Condensed: Book 3"
6.) "The Law of One- Condensed: Book 4"
7.) "The Law of One- Condensed: Book 5"

Shop for Charity:
http://author-kathryn-jordyn.printify.me/

LAW of ONE- Ra Speaks: Condensed

BOOK #2 of 5.

(Easier to Read & Understand Version)

BY: Kathryn Jordyn

On January 15th, 1981 a research group (Don, Carla and Jim) started receiving a communication from the social memory complex, Ra. Don, the questioner; Carla, the channeler; Jim, the scribe. From this communication precipitated the Law of One and some distortions of the Law of One. Book 2 contains the communications received in sessions 27-50 with Ra. Book 2 of the Law of One builds very carefully on concepts received during the first 26 sessions with Ra. This book concentrates on the metaphysical principles which govern our spiritual evolution as we seek to understand and use catalyst of our daily experiences. A more thorough examination of the energy centers of the body, and the connections between mind, body and spirit, is carried out, building upon information received in the first 26 sessions. The group learns more about Wanderers, the various densities, healing, and the many energy exchanges and blockages native to our illusion relating to experiences such as sex, illness, and meditation.

The first three sessions of Book 2 (27-29) may be difficult and confusing to anyone not familiar with the system of physics authored by Dewey B. Larson. Don't be discouraged, since Larsonian physics is far from well known. Just keep reading and by session 30, you will be back on firm metaphysical ground. After finishing book 2 and going through book 1 again, book 1 will seem a lot clearer.

(I even wrote these books in such a way to make it more understandable than the transcripts of the Law of One books and cut straight to the facts, taking out all the unnecessary and repetitive conversations, which condensed it down in a much easier to read book).

The Ra contact continued for 106 sessions which were printed into four books in The Law of One series. The fifth book was all conversations with Ra I thought to be of significance, so I included those notes in book #5.

Intelligent Infinity equals one concept. To attempt to divide intelligent infinity is like attempting to divide the word faith.

Intelligent Infinity is unity. This unity is all that there is. This unity has a potential and kinetic. The potential is intelligent infinity. Tapping this potential will yield work. This work has been called by Ra, intelligent energy.

The nature of this work is dependent upon the particular distortion of free will which in turn is the nature of a particular intelligent energy of kinetic focus of the potential of unity or that which is all.

The concept of work is universal in application, as Ra uses it. Intelligent infinity has a rhythm or flow as of a giant heart beginning with the central sun, the presence of the flow inevitable as a tide of beingness without polarity, without finity; the vast and silent all beating outward, outward, focusing outward and inward until the focuses are complete. The intelligence or consciousness of foci have reached a state where their spiritual nature or mass calls them inward, inward, inward until all is coalesced. This is the rhythm of reality.

Intelligent infinity has no difference, potential or kinetic, in unity.

The basic rhythms of intelligent infinity are totally without distortion of any kind. The rhythms are clothed in mystery, for they are being itself. From this undistorted unity appears a potential in relation to intelligent energy.

In this way you may observe the term to be somewhat two-sided, one use of the term: the undistorted unity- being without any kinetic or potential side.

The other application of this term Ra uses undifferentiatedly (similarly) of the vast potential tapped into by foci or focuses of energy is intelligent energy.

Loves comes from an infinite strength of unity, the finite qualities being chosen by the particular nature of this primal movement.

The first distortion of intelligent infinity (of the Law of One) is the distortion called free will. In this distortion of the Law of One it is recognized that the Creator will know Itself.

The Creator then grants for this knowing the concept of total freedom of choice in the ways of knowing.

The experiences are the distortion of the Law of Free will or the Way of Confusion.

The Second distortion is love. Love must be defined against the background of intelligent infinity/unity/the One Creator with the primal distortion of free will. Love is the type of energy of an extremely high order which causes intelligent energy to be formed from the potential of intelligent infinity. This then may be seen to be an object rather than an activity, and the principle of this extremely strong energy focus being worshiped as the Creator instead of unity or oneness from which all Love emanates.

The vibration or density of love or understanding is not used in the same sense as the second distortion of love. The distortion of Love being the great activator and primal co-Creator of various creations using intelligent infinity.

The vibration of love being the density in which those who have learned to do a "loving" activity without significant distortion, then seek ways of light or wisdom. Then love comes into light in the sense of the activity of unity in its free will. Love uses light and has the power to direct light in its distortions. Thus, vibratory complexes recapitulate (repeats) in reverse the great creation in its unity, thus showing the rhythm or flow of the great heartbeat.

The physics of Dewey Larson says all is motion which we can take as vibration, and that vibration is pure vibration and is not physical in any way or in any form or density. The first product of that vibration is the photon or particle of light. Love creates light.

Ra says each Love, the prime movers, comes from one frequency. This frequency is unity. It is perhaps a strength than a frequency, this strength being infinite, the finite qualities being chosen by the particular nature of this primal movement.

(Love comes from an infinite strength of unity, the finite qualities being chosen by this primal movement of Love.)

This vibration is pure motion and pure love. It is nothing that is yet condensed to form any type of density of illusion. This Love then creates by this process of vibration a photon, which is the basic particle of light. This photon then, by added vibrations and rotation, further condenses into particles of the densities we experience.

The light which forms the densities has color. This color is divided into seven categories.

The nature of vibratory patterns of our universe is dependent upon the configurations placed upon the original material or light by the focus or Love using Its intelligent energy to create a certain pattern of illusions or densities in order to satisfy Its own intelligent estimate of a method of knowing Itself. Thus, the colors, are as straight, or narrow, or necessary as is possible to express, given the will of love.

There's one particular Logos, or Love, or focus of this Creator which has chosen Its natural laws and ways of expressing them mathematically.

The one undifferentiated (identical) Intelligent infinity, unpolarized, full and whole, is the macrocosm (the whole universe) of the mystery-clad being. Ra consists of the messengers of the Law of One. Unity cannot be specified by any physics but only become activated or potentiated (increase the power of or effectiveness of) intelligent infinity due to the catalyst of free will. The understandings Ra has to share begin and end in mystery.

The nature of the vibratory patterns of our universe is dependent upon the configurations placed upon the original material or light by the focus of Love using Its intelligent energy to create a certain pattern of illusions or densities in order to satisfy Its own intelligent estimate of a method of knowing Itself. The potential which then through catalyst forms the kinetic.

Ra: "This information is a natural progression of inspection of the kinetic shape of your environment. You may understand each color or ray as being a very specific and accurate portion of intelligent energy's representation of intelligent infinity, each ray having been previously inspected in other regards.

This information may be of aid here. We speak now non-specifically to increase the depth of your conceptualization (or your own idea) of the nature of what is. The universe in which you live is recapitulation (summary) in each part of intelligent infinity. Thus, you will see the same patterns repeated in physical and metaphysical areas; the rays or portions of light being, those areas of what you may call the physical illusion which rotate, vibrate, or are of a nature that may be counted or categorized in rotation manner in space/time as described by Dewey; some substances having various of the rays in a physical manifestation visible to the eye, this being apparent in the nature of your crystallized minerals which you count as precious, the ruby being red and so forth."

Light occurred as a consequence of vibration which is a consequence of Love. This light can condense into material into our density, into all of our chemical elements because of rotations of the vibration at quantized units or intervals of angular velocity.

The enabling functional focus of Love causes light to condense into our physical or chemical elements from rotational vibrations of angular velocity. The energy of Love is an ordering nature. It orders in a cumulative way from greater to lesser so that when Its universe is complete, the manner of development of each detail is inherent in the living light and thus will develop in such and such a way. Our universe having been well studied in an empirical (verifiable by observation or experiential) fashion by scientists and understood or visualized, with greater accuracy by understandings or visualizations of Dewey.

An individualized portion of consciousness is in the area of creation itself.

Ra: "You remain carefully in the area of creation itself. In this process by which free will acts upon potential intelligent infinity to become focused intelligent energy takes place without the space/time of which you are so aware as it is your continuum experience.

The experience or existence of space/time comes into being after the individuation process of Logos or Love has been completed and the physical universe has coalesced (come together to form one mass) or begun to draw inward while moving outward to the extent that which you call your sun bodies have in their turn created timeless chaos coalescing into planets, these vortices of intelligent energy spending a large amount of first density in a timeless state, the space/time realization being one of the learn/teachings of this density of beingness."

A unit of consciousness, an individualized unit of consciousness creates a unit of the creation. One individualized consciousness creates one galaxy of stars with many millions of stars in it. The possibilities are infinite. Thus, a Logos may create a solar system or it may create billions of solar systems. What we call solar system, such as our sun and 8-9 planets, Ra calls galaxy.

Our Milky Way Galaxy is a strong Logos with approximately 250 billion solar systems for Its creation. The laws or physical ways of this creation will remain constant.

We live in a lenticular Milky Way galaxy, or Star system which many people call galaxy with approximately 250 billion other suns like our own was created by a single Logos (Love/Universe).

There are many individualized portions of consciousness in this lenticular galaxy. This Logos then subdivided into more individualization of consciousness. This understanding by the questioner Ra said was perceptive and an apparent paradox.

The apparent paradox: It would seem that if one Logos creates intelligent energy ways for a large system there would not be the necessity or possibility of the further sub-Logos differentiation. However, within limits, this is precisely the case.

Ra: "In each beginning there is the beginning from infinite strength. Free will acts as a catalyst. Beings begin to form the universes. Consciousness then begins to have the potential to experience. The potentials of experience are created as a part of intelligent energy and are fixed before experience begins.

However, there is always, due to free will acting infinitely upon the creation, a great variation in initial responses to intelligent energy's potential. Thus, almost immediately the foundations of the hierarchical nature of beings begins to manifest as some portions of consciousness or awareness learn through experience in a much more efficient (or faster) manner."

Therefore, there is individualized consciousness in our lenticular galaxy that learns faster through experience and almost immediately the foundations of the hierarchical nature of beings begin so there is always mixture in densities of intelligent consciousness in the galaxy.

There are some portions of consciousness that learn more quickly and are more efficient in learning. There's a function of the will of attraction to the upward spiraling line of light.

When this major galaxy was created, the eight densities were created as well. However, the 8th density functions also as the beginning density of first density, in its latter stages, of the next octave of densities.

Ra can speak of their experiences and understandings in limited ways. However, they cannot speak in firm knowledge of all the creations. They know only that they are infinite, so they assume an infinite number of octaves.

Their own teachers impressed upon them that there is a mystery-clad unity of creation in which all consciousness periodically coalesces (joins together into one mass) and again begins. Ra assumes an infinite progression though they understand it to be cyclical in nature and clad (clothed) in mystery.

When the galaxy is formed by the Logos, electrical polarity in the way Larson stipulated (specified) its meaning but also in the metaphysical sense. There was also polarity in consciousness.

All is potentially available from the beginning of our physical space/time, it then being the function of consciousness complexes (of free will) to begin to use the physical materials to gain experience to then polarize in a metaphysical sense. The potentials for this are not created by the experiencer but by intelligent energy.

The process of creation, after the original creation of the galaxy, is continued by further individualization of the consciousness of the Logos so that there are many, many portions of the individualized consciousness creating further items for experience all over the galaxy.

Within the guidelines or ways of the Logos, the sub-Logos may find various means of differentiating experiences without removing or adding to these ways.

Session 29: 2-23-1981

Our sun is a physical manifestation of a sub-Logos.

The sub-Logos of our solar entity differentiated (recognized the difference between) some experiential components within the patterns of intelligent energy set in motion by the Logos which created the basic conditions and vibratory rates consistent throughout our major galaxy.

Our sun is a sub-Logos of the Logos of our major Milky Way Galaxy.

A sub-sub-Logos is you, a mind/body/spirit complex.

Every entity that exists would be some type of sub or sub-sub-Logos, down to the limits of any observation, for the entire creation is alive.

A planet is named only as Logos if It is working in harmonic fashion with entities or mind/body complexes upon Its surface or within Its electromagnetic field.

Entities through the level of planets have the strength of intelligent infinity through the use of free will, going through the actions of beingness. The creation of the One Infinite Creator does not have the positive or negative terms of polarity.

It is only when the planet begins harmonically interacting with mind/body/spirit complexes, that planets take on distortions due to the thought complexes of entities interacting with the planetary entity, such as planet Earth.

Planets in first density are in a timeless state to begin with. The process by which space/time (physical) comes into time/space (non-physical) continuum form is a function of the careful building of an entire or whole plan of vibratory rates, densities, and potentials. When this plan has coalesced (or combined into one mass) in the thought complexes of Love, then the physical manifestations begin to appear; this first manifestation stage being awareness or consciousness.

At the point at which this coalescence (merging to form one whole) is at the livingness or beingness point, the point or fountainhead of beginning, space/time (physical reality) then begins to unroll its scroll of livingness.

Love creates the vibration in space/time in order to form the photon. The Logos creates all densities. Quantized incremental rotations of the vibrations show up as material of these densities.

Gravity is the pressing towards the inner light/love, the seeking towards the spiral line of light which progresses towards the Creator. This is a manifestation of a spiritual event or condition of livingness.

The gravity on our moon is less than it is on Earth. The metaphysical and physical are inseparable. The phenomenon is able to calculate the gravitational force of most objects due to various physical aspects such as mass. The physical aspects of gravity correspond and is equally important to the metaphysical nature of gravity.

The attractive force, gravity, is the pressing outward force towards the Creator is greater spiritually upon the entity Venus due to the greater degree of success at seeking the Creator.

This point only becomes important when all of creation in its infinity has reached a spiritual gravitational mass of sufficient nature, the entire creation infinitely coalesces (coming together to form one mass); the light seeking and finding Its source and thusly ending the creation and beginning a new creation, such as a black hole with its conditions of infinitely great mass at the zero point from which no light may be seen as it has been absorbed.

The black hole that manifests third density is the physical complex manifestation of the spiritual or metaphysical state of the environmental material succeeding in uniting with unity or with the Creator.

When Earth is fully into fourth density, there will be a greater spiritual gravity, thus causing a denser illusion.

The increase in spiritual gravity measurable by existing instrumentation would be and will be statistical in nature only and not significant.

As the rotations of the vibration which is light forms the atoms that forms creation, they coalesce (or combine together) in a certain manner sometimes. The precise crystalline structure formation from intelligent energy shows that it is possible by some technique to tap intelligent energy and bring it into the physical illusion by working through the crystalline structure must be charged by a correspondingly crystallized or regularized or balanced mind/body/spirit complex.

Each mind/body/spirit complex is a unique portion of the One Creator.

The necessity is for the mind/body/spirit complex to be of a certain balance, this balance enabling it to reach a set level lack of distortion. The critical difficulties are unique for each mind/body/spirit complex due to the experiential distillations (clear understanding of the past) which in total are the violet-ray beingness of each entity.

This balance is what is necessary for work to be done in seeking the gateway to intelligent infinity through the use of crystals or through any other use. No two mind/body/spirit crystallized natures are the same. The distortion requirements, vibrationally speaking, are set.

Reading the violet ray of an entity determines whether the entity could use crystals to tap intelligent energy. It is possible for 5th density or above to do this.

The gateway to intelligent infinity is born of the sympathetic vibration (occurring when an object vibrates in response to a sound wave that has the same frequency) in balanced state accompanying the will to serve, the will to seek.

The use of crystal in physical manifestation is that use wherein the entity of crystalline nature charges the regularized physical crystal with this seeking, enabling it to vibrate harmonically and also become the catalyst or gateway whereby intelligent infinity may become intelligent energy, this crystal serving as an analog (comparable) of the violet ray of the mind/body/spirit in relatively undistorted form.

There are things Ra considers not efficacious (not effective) to tell people due to possible infringement upon free will. Entities of the Confederation have done this in the past. The uses of the crystal include the uses for healing, for power, and even for the development of lifeforms. Ra feels that it is unwise to offer instruction at this time on specific uses of crystals, as people have shown a tendency to use powerful sources of power for disharmonious reasons.

Our particular Logos of our major galaxy has used a large portion of its coalesced material to reflect the beingness of the Creator. In this way there is much of our galactic system which does not have the progression of developing into higher density planets, but dwells spiritually as a portion of the Logos. Of those entities upon which consciousness dwells there is a variety of time/space periods during which the higher densities of experience are attained by consciousness.

Session 30: 2-24-1981

Creation is a single entity or unity. If only a single entity exists, then the only concept of service is the concept of service to self. If this entity subdivides, then the concept of service of one of its parts to one of its other parts is born. From this, springs the equality of service to self or to others.

Polarities begin to be explored only at the point when a third density entity becomes aware of the possibility of choice between the concept or distortion of service to self or service to others. This marks the end of the unselfconscious or innocent phase of conscious awareness.

Mind, body, and spirit are all simplistic terms which equal a complex of energy focuses:

-The body- being the material of the density which you experience at a given space/time or time/space. This complex of materials being available for distortions of physical manifestation.

-The mind- is a complex which reflects the in-pourings of the spirit and the up-pourings of the body complex. It contains feelings, emotions and intellectual thoughts in its more conscious complexities.

Ra: "Moving further down the tree of mind we see the intuition which is of the nature of the mind more in contact or in tune with the total beingness complex. Moving down to the roots of mind we find the progression of consciousness which gradually turns from the personal to the racial memory, to the cosmic influxes, and thus become a direct contactor of that shuttle which we call the spirit complex.

This spirit complex is the channel whereby the in-pourings from all of the various universal, planetary, and personal in-pourings may be funneled into the roots of consciousness and whereby consciousness may be funneled to the gateway of intelligent infinity through the balanced intelligent energy of body and mind.

You will see by this series of definitive statements that mind, body, and spirit are inextricably (impossible to separate) intertwined and cannot continue, one without the other. Thus, we refer to the mind/body/spirit complex rather than attempting to deal with them separately, for the work that you do during your experiences is done through the interaction of these three components, not through any one (of these)."

Upon our physical death from third density and this particular incarnative experience, we lose this chemical body. Immediately after the loss of this chemical body we maintain a mind/body/spirit complex.

The physical body complex we now associate with the term being but manifestation of a more dense and intelligently informed and powerful body complex.

During the transition that humans call death there is a great loss of mind complex due to that fact that much of the activity of the mental nature that we are aware during our experience of this space/time continuum is as much of a surface illusion as the chemical body complex.

((In other words, there is a great loss of mind complex from the veil of forgetting between the conscious and unconscious mind that creates an illusion of separation of our experiential awareness on Earth. Then, it transitions to true reality after death of what true reality is. This is also what the illusion means.))

In other terms, nothing whatsoever of importance is lost; the character or pure distillation of emotions and biases or distortions and wisdoms becoming obvious for the first time. These pure emotions and wisdoms and bias/distortions being, for the most part, either ignored or underestimated during physical life experience.

The spiritual channel is then much opened due to the lack of necessity for the forgetting characteristic of third density.

Mind, body, spirit originates through evolution. The consciousness in first density being without movement, a random thing. Ra says whether we call this a mind or body complex is a semantic (interpretation) problem. A semantic problem is technically meaning the same thing, but each entity may analyze and study each word or phrase for their meaning. Ra calls it mind/body complex recognizing always that in the simplest iota of this complex exists in its entirely the One Infinite Creator.

The mind/body complex in 2nd density discovers the growing and turning towards the light, thus awakening what you may call the spirit complex, that which intensifies the upward spiraling towards the love and light of the Infinite Creator.

The addition of this spirit complex having existed potentially from the beginning of space/time, perfects itself by graduation into third density. When the mind/body/spirit complex becomes aware of the possibility of service to self or other self, then the mind/body/spirit complex is activated.

On Earth during 2nd density there was habitation during the same space/time of bipedal entities (beings standing upright) with the dinosaurs. These two types of entities seemed very incompatible with each other. They both inhabited the same space/time during second density because of the workings of free will as applied to evolution. There are paths the mind/body complex follows in an attempt to survive, to reproduce, and to seek in its fashion what is unconsciously felt as the potential for growth. These two arenas or paths of development being two among many.

=>Bisexual reproduction first originates in 2nd density.

=>The second density is the groundwork being laid for third density work. In this way it may be seen that the basic mechanism of reproduction capitulates (surrenders) into a vast potential in third density for service to other self and to self; this being not only by functions of energy transfer, but also by the various services performed due to close contact of those magnetically attracted to one another; these entities thus having the opportunities for many types of service unavailable to the independent entity.

Increasing the opportunity of the experience of the One Creator is the key that occurs in all densities.

The bisexual reproduction or the philosophy of it plays a part in the spiritual growth of second density entities in isolated instances due to efficient perceptions upon the part of entities or species. For the greater part, by far, this is not the case in second density, the spiritual potentials being those of third density.

Metaphysical descriptions of planets within our solar system that have individual mind/body/spirit complexes have been, are or shall be experienced are listed below. The other planets not listed are part of the Logos.

Venus-This planetary sphere was of rapid evolution. It is Ra's native Earth and the rapidity of the progress of mind/body/spirit complexes upon its surface was due to harmonious interaction.

Mars- This entity, as already discussed, was stopped mid-third density, thus being unable to continue in progression due to lack of hospitable conditions upon the surface. This planet shall be undergoing healing for some of our space/time millennia.

Earth- This planet which we dwell on has a metaphysical history well known to us in early portions of this content.

Saturn- Was a great affinity (fondness) for the infinite intelligence and thus it has been dwelled upon in its magnetic fields of time/space by those who wish to protect our solar system. (Council of 9 or the Guardians).

Uranus- Is slowly moving through first density and has the potential of moving through all densities.

Therefore, Mercury, Jupiter, Neptune and Pluto not listed by Ra is because these planets are a part of the Logos and do not have living entities on them. Even Uranus in first density has entities in first density such as water, Earth, wind and fire that still has potential to evolve through all densities.

These planets, however, is a part of the major galactic system dwelling spiritually as part of the Logos.

The Logos has distributed itself throughout our galactic system. However, the time/space continua of some of our more central sun systems are much further advanced.

The spiritual density or mass of those more towards the center of our galaxy is known. However, this is due to the varying timelessness states during which planets may coalesce (come together to form one mass), this process of space/time beginning occurring earlier as you approach the center of the galactic spiral.

Session 31: 2-25-1981

Sexual Positive or Negative Energy Transfers or Blockages:

-1st energy center Transfer= Red ray. Random transfer having only to do with our reproductive system.

-The orange and yellow ray=Attempts to have sexual intercourse and creates a blockage if only one entity vibrates in this area, thus causing the entity vibrating sexually in this area to have a never-ending appetite for this activity (by not giving their partner an orgasm). What these vibratory levels are seeking is green ray activity.

The possibility of orange or yellow ray energy transfer polarizes negative if one is being seen as an object rather than

23

other self; the other seeing itself as plunderer or master of the situation.

(I always knew it seemed of the negative polarity for someone to just see someone as an object, with no love and just wanted to control the situation. Just because they were "straight" didn't make it positively oriented. It always felt more negative for people just to use each other for sex and view the others as an object instead of caring about them, getting to know the person and forming a loving relationship with them. The loving sexual relationship would be the green ray positive activity. That's why I chose females more often because of the love they had for me, whereas most guys just viewed me as an object and I didn't want that. I wanted the positive green ray sexual polarity and gender didn't matter, just the romantic and emotional connection did to me.)

Ra says in green ray there are two possibilities.

One: If both vibrate in green ray there will be a mutually strengthening energy transfer, the negative (female) drawing the energy from the roots of the beingness through the energy centers, thus being physically revitalized.

Two: The positive (male polarity) as deemed in our illusion, finding in its energy transfer an inspiration which satisfies and feeds the spirit portion of the body/mind/spirit complex, thus both being polarized and releasing the excess each has in abundance by nature of intelligent energy. That is, negative/intuitive, positive/physical energies; this energy transfer being blocked if one or both entities have fear of possession or of being possessed sexually, of desiring sexual possession or desiring being possessed physically or sexually by the other.

The other green-ray possibility is that of one entity offering green-ray energy, the other not offering energy of the universal love energy, this resulting in a blockage of energy for the one not green ray; the green ray being polarizing slightly towards service to others. The one not acting sexually in service to the other in universal love may gain negative polarity.

The blue ray energy transfer is somewhat rare among people on Earth, at least in 1981, but is of great aid due to energy transfers involved in becoming able to express the self without reservation or fear.

The indigo-ray transfer is extremely rare among our people on Earth. This is the sacramental portion of the body complex where contact may be made through violet ray with intelligent infinity. No blockages may occur at these latter two levels due to the fact that if both entities are not ready for this energy it is not visible and neither transfer nor blockage may take place. It is as though the distributor were removed from a powerful engine.

Energy transfer implies the release of potential energies across a potentiated (more effective) space. The sexual energy transfers occur due to the polarizations of two mind/body/spirit complexes, each of which have some potential difference one to the other. The nature of the transfer of energy or of blockage is the interaction of these two potentials. A transfer taking place is like a circuit being closed. You may also see this activity, as all experiential activities, as the Creator experiencing Itself.

Ra: "This is 'one appropriate' way the Creator knowing Itself, for in each interaction, no matter what the distortion, the Creator is experiencing Itself. The bisexual (dual) knowing of the Creator by Itself has the potential for two advantages.

Firstly, in the green-ray activated being there is the potential for a direct and simple analog (comparable) of joy, the spiritual or metaphysical nature which exists in intelligent energy. This is a great aid to comprehension of a truer nature of beingness. The other potential advantage of bisexual reproductive acts is the possibility of a sacramental understanding or connection with the gateway to intelligent infinity, for with appropriate preparation, work in magic may be done and experiences of intelligent infinity may be had. Bisexual reproduction is the reproduction between two people, it has nothing to do with being bisexually attracted to both male and female. Even though it is not wrong if one was. It's

25

the free will choice of each entity who they are attracted to, as long as they do not infringe on the free will choices of others.

The positively oriented individuals concentrating upon this method of reaching intelligent infinity, then, through the seeking or the act of will, are able to direct this infinite intelligence to the work these entities desire to do, whether it be knowledge of service or ability to heal or whatever service to others is desired.

These are two advantages of this particular method of the Creator experiencing Itself. As we have said before, the corollary (immediate consequence) of the strength of this particular energy transfer is that it opens the door to the individual mind/body/spirit complexes' desire to serve in an infinite number of ways of an other-self, thus polarizing towards positive."

Ra: "The sexual energy transfers include the red ray transfer which is random and which is a function of the second-density attempt to grow, to survive. This is a proper function of the sexual interaction. The offspring, as you call the incarnated entity, takes on the mind/body/spirit complex opportunity offered by this random act or event called the fertilization of egg by seed which causes an entity to have the opportunity to then enter this density as an incarnate entity.

This gives the two who were engaged in this bisexual reproductive energy transfer the potential for great service in this area of the nurturing of the small entities (children) as it gains in experience.

It shall be of interest at this point to note that there is always the possibility of using these opportunities to polarize towards the negative, and this has been aided by the gradual building up over many thousands of your years of social complex distortions which create a tendency towards confusion or baffling of the service to others aspect of this energy transfer and subsequent opportunities for service to other selves."

There is always the red-ray energy transfer due to the nature of the body complex. This random result of energy transfer will be the possibility of fertilization at a given time in a given pairing of entities each entity being undistorted in any vital sense by the yellow or orange ray energies; thus, the gift being given freely, no payment requested either of body, of mind, or of the spirit. The green ray is complete universality of love. This is a given without expectation of return.

A couple having a child or not is random within certain limits. If an entity has reached the seniority where it chooses the basic structure of the life experience, they may choose to incarnate in a physical body not capable of reproduction. Thus, some entities choose to be infertile. Other entities, through free will, make use of various devices to insure nonfertility. Except for these conditions, the condition is random.

Ra used the term magnetic attraction to indicate that in our bisexual natures there is polarity of male/female polarization of each entity, be each entity biologically male or female. Thus, the magnetism which two entities with the appropriate balance, male/female verses female/male polarity, meeting and feeling the attraction which polarized forces will exert, one upon the other.

This is the strength of the bisexual mechanism. It does not take an act of will to decide to feel attraction for one who is oppositely polarized sexually. (Gay people may feel opposite attraction in the sense of one person being feminine and the other being more masculine.) It will occur in an inevitable sense, giving the free flow of energy a proper avenue. This avenue may be blocked by some distortion toward a belief/condition stating to the entity that this attraction is not desired. However, the basic mechanism functions as simply as would the magnet of the iron.

Homosexual entities have experienced many incarnations as biological male and as biological female. This would not suggest what you call homosexuality in an active phase if not for the difficult vibratory condition of your planetary sphere. There is what you may call great aura infringement among your crowded urban areas in your more populous countries.

Ra: "The bisexual reproductive urge has as its goal, not only the simple reproductive function, but more especially the desire to serve others being awakened by this activity.

In an over-crowded situation where each mind/body/spirit complex is under constant bombardment from other selves it is understandable that those who are especially sensitive would not feel the desire to be of service-to-other selves. This would also increase the probability of a lack of desire or a blockage of the red ray reproductive energy.

In an uncrowded atmosphere this same entity would, through the stimulus of feeling the solitude about it, then have much more desire to seek out someone to whom it may be of service, thus regularizing the sexual reproductive function."

Jordyn says: "There are those LGBT people of seniority of vibration or certain Wanderers who many not have the desire for reproduction, thus, not needing the opposite gender for reproduction purposes. Or there are those LGBT people who do want to reproduce, but only with someone they love, thus, only pursuing an emotional connection that may be male or female. They want to serve the one they love and that person may be of the same gender. As many males are attracted to females' femininity. Certain LGBT people may be attracted to the masculine energy and vice versa. I know with me personally I want to find that romantic and emotional connection. I've mainly felt the emotional connection with other females so that's who I go for. I can still serve her through reproducing with her. It's about love, not using the opposite gender to produce a baby. That would be selfish in my eyes, or it's selfish if someone pursues the opposite gender for sexual reasons, without any emotional attachment to them."

Kathryn's question Channeled: "Is transgender okay to transition medically from female to male?"

Answer: "The transition from one physical vehicle is a complex matter of an entities free will and unique life stream, so maybe furthering their path by such transition while others may

28

not. It is important that the aspect of evaluation of each case by the polarization of an entities inner motivations and intensions is important. Furthermore, the goal is to ever align with the premise of service-to-others expansion of the one creation. As the highest wisdom is to see the One Creator within all beings and trust in the perfect unfolding of each entities journey amid the greater cosmic plan." In conclusion, it is each person's free will to choose whether they want to transition or not. Their inner motivation and intensions is what's important and whether its aligned with serving others or not. Therefore, if they still desire to serve others after their transition, then their free will choice to transition is okay as the One Creator is in all beings, even those that transition.

No gender on certain planets:

Certain planets do not have genders. Our planet has masculinity, femininity and some are in the middle. Those that incarnated into a male body is for the purpose of balancing masculine energy and mastering the masculine energy, as the past incarnation cycle most likely was a feminine type. Because the lessons of balancing the masculine and feminine is the most important lesson that each person has to learn. There are also those in the middle who are here to learn the lessons of masculine and feminine at the same time (I believe that would be me).

Kathryn channels and asks: "How is sexuality a false sense of identity?"

Higher Self answer: "At birth a sexuality isn't known. The societal complex comes up with these names, therefore sexuality is a false sense of identity. If the entity is devoid of any type of physical bodily complex or any type of thought form, there will be no objectification and identification with any type of concept, which indeed may be considered as a false sense of identity, like the naming symbolism is a false sense of identity, since many entities are named after birth. However, at the time of birth the naming concept is not present. Indeed, the symbolism of names can also be considered as a false sense of identity. And any aspect generated by the mind complex is a false sense of identity. Which takes the self away from the true nature of reality of unification of all beings."

Kathryn channels and asks: "Is homosexuality okay if they don't have an emotional connection with the opposite gender?"

Higher Self answer: "We must firstly state that this is primarily the choice of the entities involved. It is the free will which entities can experience and explore if they desire."

Kathryn channels and asks: "Will homosexuality lower an entities positive polarity?" (This question is important, because 51% positive polarity is needed to graduate to the 4th Density New Earth in 2030.)

Higher Self answer: "The answer is incorrect. We must state that the aspect of homosexuality does not have any effect on an entity's polarization, but it's actions which determine the positive polarity or negative polarity of the entity." (Therefore, it's the actions that determines the positive or negative polarity, not the sexuality. Thus, gay people will be in the 4th density New Earth who are at least 51% positively oriented service to others.)

Book 2 continues:

A male would have had roughly 65% of its incarnations in the sexual/biological body complex of a female to have a highly homosexual orientation in this incarnation, and vice versa with females having roughly 65 percent of its past incarnations as a biological male body to be of a highly homosexual orientation.

Ra: "It is to be noted at this juncture that although it is much more difficult, it is possible in this type of association for an entity to be of great service to another in fidelity and sincere green ray love of a nonsexual nature."

Kathryn says: "It's important to note that homosexuality is not wrong and not a sin. LGBT people can still make the 4th density harvest of 51% or more service-to-others. I'm LGBT and

I was 65% positive in 2023 and now 68% positive in 2024, so I'm definitely harvestable for 4th density even when I date women. By June 2024 my positive polarity was 87%."

Ra also states that masturbation and homosexuality is often innocent exercises in curiosity.

Due to solitary sexual experiences, in most cases it is unlikely masturbation has an imprinting effect upon later experiences. This is similarly true of some of the encounters which might be seen as homosexual among those of earlier sexual experiences. That these are often innocent exercises in curiosity.

However, the first sexual experience someone is involved in will indeed imprint upon the entity for that life experience a set of preferences. Therefore, if the first sexual experience is of the same gender, that entity may prefer the same gender for the remainder of their life.

Just as the Confederation attempts to beam their love and light whenever given the opportunity, including sexual opportunities, so the Orion group will use an opportunity to beam negatively orientated energy to influence those sexually towards service-to-self or if the entity is negatively oriented, the negative beings will continue to influence these beings towards greater service-to-self even through sexual acts.

The sexual energy buildup is extremely unlikely to occur without sexual bias from the entity. It would take an entity with the potential for sexual activity to experience a sexual energy buildup.

Even negatively oriented sexual experiences have the potential for sexual energy buildup.

Even negatively oriented sexual experiences have the potential for sexual energy buildup. The choice of stimulus is the choice of the entity. Members of the Third Reich had reports of sexual gratification from the observation of the gassing and killing of entities in the gas chambers. These entities were strongly polarized orange ray, thus finding the energy blockage of power over others, the putting to death being the ultimate power over others; this then being expressed in a sexual manner, though solitary. This is negatively oriented. In this case the desire would continue unabated (persistently) and be virtually unquenchable (unsatisfied).

The entire spectrum of sexual practices among people on Earth, that those who experience gratification from domination over others either from rape or other means of domination. In each case is an example of energy blockage sexual in its nature. Of course, negatively oriented as well.

The cause of this is not Orion. It is the free choice of people on Earth.

The sexual energy transfers and blockages are more of a manifestation or example that is more fundamental than the other way about. Therefore, as people become open to bellicosity (which is a person's tendency to fight) and the greed of ownership, these various distortions then began to filter down through the tree of mind into sexual expressions. Thus, these sexual energy blockages, though Orion influenced and intensified, are basically the product of the beingness chosen freely by people.

The racial memory contains all that has been experienced. Thus, there is some contamination even of the sexual, this showing mostly in our own culture on Earth as the various predispositions to adversary relationships or marriages, rather than the free giving one to another in the love and the light of the Infinite Creator.

Session 32: 2-27-1981

Orange ray activation is that influence or vibratory pattern wherein the mind/body/spirit expresses its power on an individual basis. Power over individuals may be seen to be orange ray. This ray has been quite intense among people on Earth on an individual

32

basis. You may see in this ray treating other selves as non-entities, slaves, or chattel, thus giving other selves no status whatsoever.

The yellow ray is a focal and very powerful ray and concerns the entity in relation to groups, societies or large numbers of people. This yellow ray vibration is at the heart of bellicose actions (which is someone wishing to fight or start a war) in which one group of entities feels the necessity and right of dominating other groups of entities and bending their will to the wills of the masters.

The negative path uses a combination of the yellow ray and the orange ray in its polarization patterns. These rays, used in a dedicated fashion, will bring about a contact with intelligent infinity. The usual nature of sexual interaction, if one is yellow or orange in primary vibratory patterns, is one of blockage and then insatiable hunger due to the blockage. When there are two selves vibrating in this area the potential for polarization through sexual interaction is begun, one entity experiencing the pleasure of humiliation and slavery or bondage, the other experiencing the pleasure of mastery and control over another entity. This way a sexual energy transfer of negative polarity is experienced.

Green ray energy transfer is the turning point sexually as well as in each other mode of experience. The green ray may then be turned outward, the entity then giving rather receiving. The first giving beyond green ray is the giving of acceptance or freedom, thus allowing the recipient of blue ray energy transfer the opportunity for a feeling of being accepted, which frees that other self to express itself to the giver of this ray.

Once green ray energy transfer has been achieved by two mind/body/spirits complexes in mating, the further rays are available without both entities having the necessity to progress equally.

A blue ray vibrating entity or indigo ray vibrating entity whose other ray vibrations are clear may share that energy with the green ray other self, thus acting as catalyst for the continued learn/teaching of the other self. Until an other-self reaches green ray, such energy transfer through the rays is not possible.

The indigo ray is the ray of awareness of Creator as self; thus, one whose indigo ray vibrations have been activated can offer the energy transfer of Creator to Creator. This is the beginning of the sacramental nature of the bisexual reproductive act. It is unique in bearing the allness, the wholeness, the unity in its offering to other self.

The violet ray, just as the red ray, is constant in the sexual experience. Its experience by other self may be distorted or completely ignored or not apprehended by other self. However, this ray, being the sum and substance of mind/body/spirit complex, surrounds and informs any action by a mind/body/spirit complex.

The rays have such a different meaning in the next density and the higher densities. Energy transfers only take place in fourth, fifth and sixth densities. These are still a polarized nature. However, due to the ability of these densities to see harmonies between individuals, these entities choose mates that are harmonious, thus allowing constant energy transfer and the propagation (increase in individuals or spreading) of the body complexes each density uses. Even creating more humans. The process is different in the fifth and sixth density. However, it is in these cases still based upon polarity.

The seventh density does not have the sexual energy exchange as it is unnecessary to recycle body complexes.

Ra: "Fourth-density Wanderers, of which there are not many, will tend to choose those entities which seem to be full of love or in need of love. There is the great possibility/probability of entities making errors in judgment due to the compassion with which other selves are viewed.

The fifth-density Wanderer is one who is not tremendously affected by the stimulus of the various rays of other self and in its

34

own way offers itself when a need is seen. Such entities are not likely to engage in the custom of your people called marriage and are very likely to feel an aversion to childbearing and child raising due to the awareness of the impropriety of the planetary vibrations (which is the dishonest or unacceptable behavior on the planet relative to the harmonious vibrations of the density of light.)

The sixth density, whose means of propagation (or reproduction) you may liken to what you call fusion, is likely to refrain, to a great extent, from the bisexual reproductive programming of the bodily complex and instead seek out those with whom the sexual energy transfer is of the complete fusion nature in so far as this is possible in manifestation in third density."

The entire creation is of the One Creator. Thus, the division of sexual activity into the body is an artificial division, all things being seen as sexual equally, the mind, the body, and the spirit; all of which are part of the polarity of the entity. Thus, sexual fusion may be seen with or without sexual intercourse to be the complete melding of the mind, the body and the spirit in what feels to be a constant orgasm of joy and delight in the other's beingness.

The possibility/probability of many Wanderers having considerable problems with 3rd density incarnation being of a different sexual ray energy is rather large. The problem depends upon each unique orientation of each mind/body/spirit complex having this situation or placement of vibratory relativities.

The vibration of the different energy ray colors may be seen to have mathematically straight or narrow steps. These steps may be seen as having boundaries. Within each boundary there are infinite gradations (which is the minute changes) of vibration of color.

As one approaches a boundary, an effort must be made to cross that boundary division of our density. There is also the time/space analogy which may be seen as the color itself in a modified aspect.

The green ray activation is always vulnerable to the yellow or orange ray of possession, this being largely yellow ray but often coming into orange ray.

Fear of possession, desire for possession, fear of being possessed, desire to be possessed are distortions that will cause the deactivation of green-ray energy transfer.

Once the green ray has been achieved, the ability of the entity to enter blue ray is immediate and is only awaiting the efforts of the individual. The indigo ray is opened only through considerable discipline and practice largely having to do with acceptance of self, not only as polarized and balanced self but as Creator and of infinite worth. This will begin to activate the indigo ray.

Session 33: 3-1-1981

(How Ra normally starts each session).

Ra: "I am Ra. I greet you in the love and the light of the One Infinite Creator. I communicate now."

When looking out for the vital energies necessary for non-depletion of the instrument and the contact level: Each entity is responsible for itself. However, Ra would always end a session when the instruments energies was low or the pain level was increasing due to her arthritis. This was to avoid depleting the instrument. The group must voice any concerns if needed. The instrument needs to watch its vital energies, for Ra does not wish to deplete the instrument.

The function of the supporting group may be of protection for the Ra contact and they may energize the instrument and intensify its vital energies. The supporting group being Don Elkins the questioner and Jim the Scribe.

This supporting group has always provided protection in love and light due to an underlying harmony, thus ensuring the continuation of the narrow band contact. However, the vital energies of either of the supporting members being depleted, the instrument must then use a larger portion of its vital energies, thus depleting itself more than would be profitable on a long-term basis.

How to maintain the best possible condition for maintaining contact: Ra suggests rather than being brave and ignoring a physical weakness that it is good to share the distortion with the group and perhaps remove one opportunity for contact which is very wearying for the instrument, in order that another opportunity might come about in which the instrument is properly supported and feeling better.

Secondly, the work begun in harmony may continue in harmony, thanksgiving and praise of opportunities of the Creator. These are your protections. These are Ra's suggestions. Ra cannot be specific for their free will is the essence of the contact. Ra only states this because of Ra's grasp of the (channeling) group's desires for long-term maintenance of the contact. This is acceptable to Ra.

The color therapy device is the shining of particular colors on the physical body is a somewhat clumsy and variably useful tool for instigating in an entity's mind/body/spirit complex an intensification of energies or vibrations which may be of aid to the entity.

The variableness (changeability) of this device is due to the lack of true colors used and to extreme variation in sensitivity to vibration among our peoples on Earth.

One way of approaching accuracy in color would be passing light through a crystal of the particular color. This is not a great or even visible variation; however, it does make some difference given specific applications.

One could possibly use a prism breaking white light into its spectrum and screening off all parts of the spectrum except what you wish to use by passing it through a slit.

The incarnating entity which has become conscious of the incarnative process and thus programs its own experience may choose the amount of catalyst or the number of lessons it will undertake to experience and to learn from in one incarnation.

Not all is predestined, but there are invisible guidelines shaping events which will function according to this programming. Thus, if one opportunity is missed another will appear until the student of the life experience grasps that a lesson is being offered and undertakes to learn it.

These lessons would be reprogrammed as the life experience continues. Let's say that an entity develops the bias that he actually didn't choose to develop prior to incarnation. It is then possible to program experiences so that he will have an opportunity to alleviate this bias through balancing.

To the best of Ra's knowledge: The orientation or polarization of the mind/body/spirit complex is the cause of the perceptions generated by each entity.

An example observed in your grocery store: The entity ahead of self may be without sufficient funds. One entity may take this opportunity to steal. Another may feel itself a failure. Another may unconcernedly remove the least necessary items, pay for what it can, and go about its business. The one observing may feel compassion. Another observing may feel an insult because of standing next to a poverty-stricken person. Another observing may feel indifference. The other observing may feel generosity. These are analogies (the comparison between two or more things for clarification).

Fourth-density positive has the concept of defensive action, but above fourth density defensive action is not in use due to the wisdom density. The concept of defensive and offensive action is very much in use in our 3rd density Earth.

In each case, an entity able to program experiences may choose the number and the intensity of lessons to be learned. It is possible that an extremely positive oriented entity might program for itself situations testing the ability of self to refrain from defensive action even to the point of physical death of self or other self. This is an intensive lesson and it is not known what entities have programmed. Ra may read the programming if they desire. However, they choose not to because it is an infringement.

The movie, the Ninth Configuration, the Colonel made the decision to defend his friend instead of allowing his friend to be suppressed by the negatively oriented entities. This is an action of 3rd or 4th density seen by the action of Jehoshuah, which many people on Earth refer to as Jesus. Jehoshuah was to be defended by its friends. Jehoshuah reminded its friends to put away the sword. This entity then delivered itself to be put to the physical death. The impulse to protect the loved other self is one which persists through the fourth density, a density abounding in compassion. More than this Ra cannot and need not say.

The planetary catastrophes are a symptom of the difficult harvest rather than a consciously programmed catalyst for harvest. Thus, Ra does not concern themselves with it, for it is random in respect to conscious catalyst such as Ra makes available.

The results of the random catalyst of the Earth changes are also random. Thus, Ra may see probability/possibility vortices going towards positive and negative. However, it will be as it will be. The true opportunities for conscious catalyst are not the Earth changes but the result of the seniority system of incarnations are those who placed in incarnation who have the best chance of using their life experiences to become harvestable.

This seniority system is also used in the service-to-self. Other catalytic influences are the Creator's universe and the self-service for becoming harvestable negatively.

The primary mechanism (or piece in a larger process) for catalytic experience in third density is other self (other beings). Other catalytic influences are the Creator's universe and the self.

The self-acted upon catalytically that produces experience: Firstly, the self-unmanifested. Secondly, the self in relation to the societal self-created by self and other self. Thirdly, the interaction between self and the gadgets, toys, and amusements of the self, other self-invention. Fourthly, the self-relationship with those attributes of war and rumors of war. An example of unmanifested self is physical pain. The self not needing other self in order to manifest or act.

Any interaction betwixt self and other self has whatever potential for catalyst that there exists in the potential difference between self and other self, this moderated and under-girded by the constant fact of the Creator as self and as other self.

The violet ray of the positive fourth density will be tinged with the green, blue, indigo triad of energies. This tinge may be seen as a portion of a rainbow or prism, the rays being quite distinct.

The violet ray of fourth-density negative has in its aura the tinge of red, orange, yellow, these rays being muddied rather than distinct.

Speaking approximately, there is a distinctive difference in the color structure of each density. 5th density is perhaps extremely white in vibration. 6th density is a whiteness which contains a golden quality as you would perceive it; these colors having to do with the blending into wisdom of the compassion learned in fourth density. Then in sixth the blending of wisdom back into a unified understanding of compassion viewed with wisdom. This golden color is not of your spectrum but is alive.

The penetration of the eighth level or intelligent infinity allows a mind/body/spirit complex to be harvested if it wishes at any time/space during the cycle.

Session 34: 3-4-1981

The experience of each entity is unique in its perception of intelligent infinity. Perceptions range from a limitless joy to a strong dedication to service to others while in the incarnated state. The entity which reaches intelligent infinity most often will perceive this experience as one of unspeakable profundity (deep insight, great depth of knowledge or thought). However, it is not usually for the entity to immediately desire the cessation of the incarnation. Rather the desire to communicate or use this experience to aid others is extremely strong.

Kathryn says: "After learning the general overview of the Law of One. I experienced this feeling, along with my prophecies. This information and my prophecies fulfilled was one of the most long-lasting, exciting feelings I ever felt. It was exciting finally finding the truth and realizing that I'm the first prophet on Earth to speak the 100% truth without the negatively influenced distortions found in half the Bible. Plus, my dreams have been the most accurate in the world as well."

Karma may be called inertia. Those actions put into motion will continue using the ways of balancing until slowed down or stopped. This stoppage of the inertia of an action is through forgiveness. These two concepts are inseparable. (Therefore, karma can be stopped through forgiveness.)

If an entity develops karma in an incarnation, programming sometimes occurs so that they may experience catalysts that will enable the entity to get to a point of forgiveness thereby alleviating the karma.

However, both self and any involved other may, at any time through understanding, acceptance, and forgiveness, ameliorate (improve) these patterns. This is true at any point in an incarnative pattern. Thus, one who has set in motion an action may forgive itself and never again make that error. This also breaks or stops karma.

The catalyst of pain is the most common experience among people on Earth. The pain may be physically more often than it is mental and emotional. In some cases, it's spiritual. This creates a potential for learning, the lessons vary. Almost always these lessons include patience, tolerance and the ability for light touch.

Very often the catalyst for emotional pain, whether it be the physical death of a loved one or other seeming loss, will simply result in the opposite, in a bitterness and impatience, a souring. This is catalyst which has gone awry. In those cases, then there will be additional catalyst provided to offer the unmanifested self-further opportunities for discovering the self as all-sufficient Creator containing all that there is and full of joy.

The unmanifested self is physical pain. The self not needing other self to manifest or act.

The so-called contagious diseases are those second density entities which offer an opportunity of catalyst for the unmanifested self (physical pain). In other words, contagious diseases are second density entities offering catalyst for the self without needing other people to manifest or act.

If this catalyst is unneeded, then these second-density creatures do not have an effect. In each of these generalizations there are anomalies so Ra can't speak to every circumstance but only to the general way of things as you experience them.

Birth defects are a portion of the programming of mind/body/spirit totality manifested in the mind/body/spirit of third density. These defects are planned as limitations which are part of the experience intended by the entity's totality complex. This includes genetic predispositions (which is an increased likelihood of developing a disease).

The unmanifested self may find its lessons with any of the energy influx centers of the mind/body/spirit complex. The societal and self-interactions most often concentrate on the 2nd and 3rd energy centers.

Those most active in attempting to remake or alter society are those working from feelings of being correct personally or having answers that will put power in a more correct configuration. This may be seen to be of full travel from negative to positive orientation. Either will activate these energy ray centers.

There are a few whose desires to aid society are green-ray or above. These entities are few due to the understanding of fourth ray that universal love freely given is more to be desired than principalities (those in governmental power like a prince) or even the rearrangement of people or political structures.

Two positively oriented active souls no longer in our physical time here on Earth are Albert Schweitzer, who went into a strange and barbaric society in order that it might heal. He was able to mobilize great amounts of energy and money. He spent much green-ray energy both as a healer and as a lover of the organ instrument. His yellow ray was bright and crystallized by the efforts needed to produce the funds to promulgate (promote) its efforts, also meaning to promote its efforts. His blue and green rays were of a toweringly brilliant nature as well. The higher levels being activated, the lower energy points remaining in balance, being quite, quite brilliant.

Another positively oriented soul strongly biased towards positive societal effects was Martin Luther King. He dealt in a great degree with rather negative orange and yellow ray vibratory patterns. However, this entity was able to keep open the green-ray energy due to the severity of its testing, this entity may be seen to have polarized more towards the positive due to its fidelity to service-to-others in the face of great catalyst.

The unmanifested self (such as physical pain)-interacting between self and gadgets, toys and inventions concentrate for the most part in the orange and yellow energy centers.

In a negative sense many of the communication devices and other distractions such as the less competitive games, may be seen to have the distortion of keeping the person unactivated so that yellow and orange ray activity is much weakened thus carefully decreasing the possibility of eventual green-ray activation.

Other gadgets seen as tools where the entity explores the capabilities of its physical or mental complexes and in a few cases, the spiritual complex, thus activating the orange ray in team sports and in modes of transport. These may be seen as investigating the feelings of power; more especially, power over others or a group power over another group of other selves.

There are many green-ray attempts of many to communicate via a T.V. for truth and beauty that may be helpful. The sum effect of this gadget is that of distraction and sleep.

This war and self-relationship are fundamental perceptions of the maturing entity. There is a great chance to accelerate in whatever direction is desired.

One may polarize negatively by assuming bellicose (hostile) attitudes, such as the tendency for fighting or war, for whatever reason.

One may find oneself in the situation of war and polarize somewhat towards the positive activating orange, yellow and then green rays by heroic actions taken to preserve the mind/body/spirit complexes of other selves.

Finally, one may polarize very strongly third ray/green ray by expressing the principle of universal love at the total expense of any distortion towards involvement in bellicose actions. In this way the entity may become a conscious being in a very brief span of your time/space. This may be a traumatic progression.

A large percentage of all entities on Earth has a progression of trauma catalyst.

Third ray is green ray. Red ray and violet ray are seen as fixed to Ra; thus, the five inner rays are the varying rays to be observed as indications of seniority in the attempts to form a harvest.

In the graduation or harvesting to fourth-density positive, the red ray is seen only as being activated, is the basis for all that occurs in vibratory levels, the sum of this being violet ray energy.

This violet ray is the only consideration for fourth density positive. In assessing the harvestable fourth-density negative, the intensity of the red, orange and yellow is looked upon quite carefully as a great deal of stamina and energy of this type is necessary for the negative progression, it being extremely difficult to open the gateway to intelligent infinity from the solar plexus center. This is necessary for harvest in fourth-density negative.

Ra: "...General George Patton, was one in whom the programming of previous incarnations had created a pattern or inertia which was irresistible in its incarnation in your time/space. This entity was of a strong yellow ray activation with frequent green ray openings and occasional blue ray openings. However, it did not find itself able to break the mold of previous traumatic experiences of a bellicose (war-like) nature.

This entity polarized somewhat towards the positive in its incarnation due to its singleness of belief in truth and beauty. This entity was quite sensitive. It felt a great honor/duty to the preservation of that which was felt by the entity to be true, beautiful, and in need of defense. This entity perceived itself a gallant figure (brave or chivalrous). It polarized somewhat towards the negative in its lack of understanding the green ray it carried with it, rejecting the forgiveness principle which is implicit (understood but not clearly expressed) in universal love.

The sum total of this incarnation vibrationally was a slight increase in positive polarity but a decrease in harvestability due to the rejection of the Law of Way of Responsibility; that is, seeing universal love, yet still it fought on."

Almost immediately after the cessation of war, General George Patton's death was so he could immediately reincarnate to make harvest.

Session 35: 3-6-1981

Ra: "It is to be noted that in discussing those who are well known among your peoples there is the possibility that information may be seen to be specific to one entity whereas in actuality the great design of experience is much the same for each entity. It is with this in mind that we would discuss the experiential forces which offered catalyst to an individual.

It is further to be noted that in the case of those entities lately incarnate much distortion may have taken place in regard to misinformation and misinterpretation of an entity's thoughts or behaviors.

We shall now proceed to speak of the basic parameters of the one known as Franklin D. Roosevelt. When any entity comes into third-density incarnation, each of its energy centers is potentiated but must be activated by the self, using experience.

The one known as Franklin developed very quickly up through red, orange, yellow, and green and began to work in the blue ray energy center at a tender age. This rapid growth was due, firstly, to previous achievements in the activation of the rays, secondly, to the relative comfort and leisure of its early existence, thirdly, due to the strong desire upon the part of the entity to progress. This entity mated with an entity whose blue ray vibrations were of a strength more than equal to its own thus acquiring catalyst for further growth in that area that was to persist throughout the incarnation.

This entity had some difficulty with continued green ray activity due to the excessive energy which was put into the activities regarding other selves in the distortion towards acquiring power. This was to have its toll upon the physical vehicle. The limitation of the nonmovement of a portion of the physical vehicle opened once again, for this entity, the opportunity for concentration upon the more, universal or idealistic aspects of power; that is, the non-abusive use of power. Thus, at the outset of a bellicose action this entity had lost some positive polarity due to excessive use of the orange and yellow ray energies at the expense of green and blue ray energies, then had regained the polarity due to the catalytic effects of a painful limitation upon the physical complex.

This entity was not of a bellicose (hostile) nature but rather during the conflict continued to vibrate in green ray working with the blue ray energies. Franklin's teacher also functioned greatly during this period as blue ray activator, not only for its mate but also in a more universal expression. This entity polarized continuously in a positive fashion in the universal sense while, in a less universal sense, developing a pattern of what may be called karma; this karma having to do with inharmonious relationship distortions with the mate/teacher."

Franklin D. Roosevelt's teacher was his wife.

He placed the physical limitations on his body himself through pre-incarnation programming.

The basic guidelines for the lessons and purposes of incarnation had been carefully set before incarnation by the mind/body/spirit complex totality of Franklin.

If he had avoided the excessive enjoyment of or attachment to the competitiveness inherent of his occupation, this entity would not have had the limitation.

However, the desire to grow was strong in this programming and when the opportunities began to cease due to distortions towards love of power the entity's limiting factor was activation.

47

There was an intense amount of confusion present in Adolf Hitler's life patterns as well as great confusion among any discussion of this entity.

Ra: "Here we see an example of one who, in attempting activation of the highest rays of energy while lacking the green ray key, canceled itself out as far as polarization either towards positive or negative. This entity was basically negative. However, its confusion was such that the personality disintegrated, thus leaving the mind/body/spirit complex unharvestable and much in need of healing.

This entity followed the pattern of negative polarization which suggests the elite and the enslaved, this being seen by the entity to be of a helpful nature for the societal structure. However, in drifting from the conscious polarization into a twilight world where dream took the place of events in your space/time continuum, this entity failed in its attempt to serve the Creator in a harvestable degree along the path of service-to-self. Thus, we see the so-called insanity which may often arise when an entity attempts to polarize more quickly than experience may be integrated.

We have advised and suggested caution and patience in previous communications and do so again, using this entity as an example of the over-hasty opening of polarization without due attention to the synthesized and integrated mind/body/spirit complex. To know your self is to have the foundation upon firm ground."

There are two entities subordinate to Adolf at the time who may be harvestable in a negative sense, one known as Hermann; the other preferred to be called Himmler. When this was channeled by Ra at the time there were others still alive harvestable 4th density negative that Ra can't mention due to them still being alive at the time of this channeling in 1981.

Ra: "This shall be the last full query of this session as we find the instrument quite low in vital energies.

The one known as Abraham (Lincoln) had an extreme difficulty in many ways and, due to physical, mental, and spiritual pain, was weary of life but without the orientation to self-destruction. In your time, 1853, this entity was contacted in sleep by a fourth-density being. This being was concerned with the battles between the forces of light and the forces of darkness which have been waged in fourth density for many of your years.

This entity accepted the honor/duty of completing Abraham's karmic patterns and Abraham discovered that this entity would attempt those things which Abraham desired to do but felt it could not. Thus, the exchange was made.

This entity, Abraham, was taken to a plane of suspension until the cessation of its physical vehicle much as though we of Ra would arrange with this instrument to remain in the vehicle, come out of the trance state, and function as this instrument, leaving this instrument's mind and spirit complex in its suspended state.

The planetary energies at this time were at what seemed to this entity to be at a critical point, for freedom had gained in acceptance as a possibility among many peoples. This entity saw the work done by those beginning the democratic concept of freedom, in danger of being abridged (shortened) or abrogated (repealed) by the rising belief and use of the principle of the enslavement of entities. This is a negative concept of a fairly serious nature in your density. This entity, therefore, went forward into what it saw as the bate for the light, for healing of a rupture in the concept of freedom.

This entity did not gain or lose karma by these activities due to its detachment from any outcome. Its attitude throughout was one of service-to-others, more especially to the downtrodden or enslaved. The polarity of the individual was somewhat, but not severely, lessened by the cumulative feelings and thought forms which were created due to large numbers of entities leaving the physical plane due to trauma of battle."

Session 36: 3-10-1981

There is a dimension in which time does not have sway (does not exist). In this dimension, the mind/body/spirit in its eternal dance of the present may be seen in totality as an eternal present, and before the mind/body/spirit complex becomes a part of the social memory complex is willingly absorbed into the allness of the One Creator, the entity knows itself in its totality.

This mind/body/spirit complex totality functions as a resource for the Higher Self. The Higher Self, in turn, is a resource for the distillations of third-density experience and programming further experience. This is also true of densities four, five and six with the mind/body/spirit complex totality coming into consciousness in the course of seventh density.

The Higher Self exists with full understanding of the accumulation of experiences of the entity, aids the entity in achieving healing of the experiences that have not been learned properly and assists in further life experience programming.

Ra: "The Higher Self exists with full understanding of the accumulation of experiences of the entity, aids the entity in achieving healing of the experiences which have not been learned properly and assists as you have indicated in further life experience programming.

The mind/body/spirit complex totality is that which may be called upon by the Higher Self aspect just as the mind/body/spirit complex calls upon the Higher Self. In the one case you have a structured situation within the space/time continuum with the Higher Self having available to it the totality of experiences which have been collected by an entity and a very firm grasp of the lessons to be learned in this density.

The mind/body/spirit complex totality is as the shifting sands and is in some part a collection of parallel developments of the same entity. This information is made available to the Higher Self aspect. This aspect may then use these projected probability/possibility vortices in order to better aid in future life programming."

Seth says in the "Seth Material" that each entity here on Earth is one part of an aspect of a Higher Self or Oversoul that has many aspects or parts in many dimensions that all learn lessons that allow the Higher Self to progress in a balanced manner.

The Higher Self governs all of our parallel realities that are similar to our experience in the third density here on Earth.

The more in balance an entity becomes, the less possibility/probability vortices may need to be explored in parallel experiences.

True simultaneity is available only when all things are seen to be occurring at once. Therefore, various parts of the being experiencing parallel experiences of varying natures is not occurring simultaneously.

From Universe to Universe and parallel existences can then be programmed by the Higher Self, given the information available from the mind/body/spirit complex totality regarding the probability/possibility vortices at any crux.

The apparent simultaneity existence of two selves is actually one-self at the same time. This oversoul or Higher Self seems to exist simultaneously with the mind/body/spirit complex that it aids. This is not actually simultaneous, for the Higher Self is moving to the mind/body/spirit complex as needed from a position in development of the entity in the future of this entity.

The Higher Self operates from the future and is aware of lessons learned through the sixth density. However, it does not know exactly what will happen in the future for that would be an abrogation (in abolishing) free will. The progress rate through sixth density is fairly well understood. The choices that must be made to achieve the Higher Self as it is are in the provenance (or birthplace) of the mind/body/spirit complex itself.

Thus, the Higher Self is like a map where the destination is known; the roads are very well known, these roads being designed by intelligent infinity working through intelligent energy. However, the Higher Self aspect can only program for the lessons and certain predisposing (or inclined towards) limitations if it wishes. The remainder is completely the free choice of each entity. There is the perfect balance between the known and the unknown.

The Higher Self does have some type of physical body. This Higher Self is of a certain advancement within sixth density going into the seventh. After the seventh has been well entered the mind/body/spirit complex becomes so totally a mind/body/spirit complex totality that it begins to gather spiritual mass and approach the octave density. Thus, the looking backwards is finished at that point.

The Higher Self of every entity is of sixth-density. This is an honor/duty of self to self as one approaches seventh density.

Each entity has several beings to call on for inner support.

The mind/body/spirit complex totality is a nebulous (or unclear/foggy) collection of all that may occur held in understanding.

The Higher Self itself is a projection or manifestation of mind/body/spirit complex totality that then may communicate with the mind/body/spirit complex during the discarnate (not having a physical body) part of a cycle of rebirth or the incarnation. It may communicate if the proper pathways or channels through the roots of mind are opened.

These channels to contact the Higher Self may be opened by meditation. Meditation also helps in evolution.

Each path of life experience is unique.

Intense polarization does not necessarily develop the will or need to contact the Oversoul. However, given the polarization, the will is greatly enhanced and vice versa.

There are no negative beings that have attained the Oversoul manifestation, which is the honor/duty of the mind/body/spirit complex totality of late sixth density. Therefore, all Higher Selves and Oversouls are of the positive polarity.

These negatively oriented mind/body/spirit complexes have a difficulty that has never been overcome. For after fifth-density graduation wisdom is available but must be matched with an equal amount of love. This love/light is very, very difficult to achieve in unity when following the negative path and during the earlier part of sixth density, society complexes of the negative orientation will choose to release the potential and leap into the sixth-density positive.

Therefore, the Oversoul which makes its understanding available to all in the social memory complex who are ready for such aid is a positive Oversoul. However, the free will of the individual is paramount, and any guidance given by a Higher Self may be seen in either the positive or negative polarity depending on the choice of the entity.

The negative path is one of separation. The first separation is the self from the self. Many negatively oriented beings choose not to use its abilities of will and polarization to seek guidance from any source but its conscious drives, self-chosen in the life experience and nourished by previous biases created in other life experiences.

Kathryn says: "I assume demons/negatively-oriented beings choosing not to seek guidance is due to separation and service-to-self choice as they are in separation and darkness."

The sixth-density negative entity is extremely wise. It observes the spiritual entropy occurring due to the lack of ability to express the unity of sixth density. Thus, loving the Creator and realizing at some point that the Creator is not only self but other self as self, this entity consciously chooses an instantaneous energy reorientation so that it may continue its evolution.

Once the negatively polarized entity has reached a certain point in the wisdom density it becomes extremely unlikely that it will choose to risk the forgetting, for this polarization is not selfless but selfish and with wisdom realizes the jeopardy of such "Wandering." Occasionally a sixth-density negative entity becomes a Wanderer in an effort to continue to polarize negatively. This is extremely unusual.

The Wanderer has the potential of greatly accelerating the density when it comes in its progress in evolution. This is due to the intensive life experiences and opportunities of third density. Thusly the positively oriented Wanderer chooses to hazard the danger of the forgetting in order to be of service to others by radiating love of others. If the forgetting is penetrated the amount of catalyst in third density will polarize the Wanderer with much greater efficiency than expected in the higher and more harmonious densities.

Similarly, the negatively oriented Wanderer dares to hazard the forgetting in order that it might accelerate its progress in evolution in its own density by serving itself in third density by offering to other selves negatively polarized information.

Examples of sixth density negatively polarized Wanderers in our historical past could be harmful Ra said. So, they withheld that information. Ra wants us to view the entities about you as part of the Creator. They can't explain any further.

Approximately 8.5-9.75% of Wanderers on Earth in the 1980's has been successful in penetrating the memory block and have become aware of who they are. About 50% have a fairly well-defined symptomology (symptoms or signs) indicating to them that they are not of this "insanity" or not of this world. Nearly one-third of the remainder are aware that something about them is different, so you see there are many gradations of awakening to the knowledge of being a Wanderer. This information will make sense to middle and first of these groups.

Session 37: 3-12-1981

Each third-density entity has a Higher Self in sixth density which is moving to the mind/body/spirit complex of the entity as needed.

The Higher Self is a manifestation given to late sixth-density mind/body/spirit complex as a gift from its future selfness. The mid-seventh density's last action before turning towards the allness of the Creator and gaining spiritual mass is to give this resource to the sixth-density self, moving as you measure time in the stream of time.

This self, the mind/body/spirit complex of late sixth density, has then the honor/duty of using both the experiences of its total living bank of memory of experience, thoughts, and actions (the Higher Self) and using the resource of the mind/body/spirit complex totality left behind from the mid-seventh density self, a type of infinitely complex thought form to give the sixth-density self as a gift.

In this way you may see yourself, Higher Self or Oversoul, and your mind/body/spirit complex totality as three points in a circle. The only distinction is that of your time/space continuum. Otherwise, all three are the same being.

Each entity has its totality and when a planetary entity becomes a social memory complex, formed in fourth-density, the totality of this union of entities also has its Oversoul and its social memory complex totality as resource. As always, the sum, spiritually speaking, is greater than the sum of its parts so that the Oversoul of a social memory complex is not the sum of the Oversouls of its members entities but operates upon the way of squares or doubling.

Spiritual mass begins to attract the out-moving and ongoing vibratory oscillations (swinging back and forth like a pendulum) of beingness into the gravity well of the great central sun, core, or Creator of the Infinite universes.

Session 38: 3-13-1981

The desire for information like nuclear energy was attracted to our people on Earth. It was not given for a reason from outside influences; rather it was desired from people on Earth. Entities desired a second chance to use nuclear energy here on Earth peacefully that caused the destruction of Maldek from nuclear energy.

Inspiration fulfilled the desire to receive the information regarding nuclear energy. This inspiration involves an extraordinary desire to know or to receive in a certain area accompanied by the ability to open to and trust in intuition.

Each balance of an entity is perfect and unique.

The rays of a Wanderer may be viewed as extremely even, red, orange, yellow and the green is extremely bright. This is balanced by a dimmer indigo.

Ra: "Between these two the point of balance resides, the blue ray of the communicator sparkling in strength above the ordinary. In the violet ray we see this unique spectrograph (which records an astronomical spectrum of all the energy rays) and at the same time the pure violet surrounding the whole; this in turn, surrounded by that which mixes the red and violet ray, indicating the integration of mind, body, and spirit; this surrounded by the vibratory pattern of this entity's true density.

This description may be seen to be both unbalanced and in perfect balance. The latter understanding is extremely helpful in dealing with other selves. The ability to feel blockages is useful only to the healer. There is not properly a tiny fraction of judgement when viewing a balance in colors. Of course, when we see many of the energy plexi weakened and blocked, we may understand that an entity has not yet grasped the baton and begun the race. However, the potentials are always there. All the rays fully balanced are there in waiting to be activated."

Perhaps another way to address this is in the fully potentiated (or effective) entity the rays mount one upon the other with equal vibratory brilliance (intense brightness of light) and scintillating sheen (shining brightly) until the surrounding color is white. This is potentiated balance in third density.

It is possible for a third-density planet to form a social memory complex in the latter or seventh portion when entities are harmoniously readying for graduation.

As far as Ra is aware there are no negatively third-density social memory complexes. Positively oriented social memory complexes of third density are not unheard of but quite rare. However, an entity from the star Sirius's planetary body has approached this planetary body twice. This entity is late third density and is part of a third-density social memory complex. The social memory complex is properly a fourth-density phenomenon.

The second-density vegetation forms that graduated into third density upon Sirius of that social memory complex third density were dogs. (Which is interesting, because dogs upon Earth are 2nd density.)

Jehoshuah was from Sirius and experienced second density life as a tree. Jehoshuah was fifth density harvestable (later fourth density) when he reincarnated as a Wanderer into third density Earth to spread love upon the Earth.

Since Bellicose is impossible for vegetation, they would then have the advantage not to carry a racial memory of a bellicose nature into third density from second and therefore develop a more harmonious society and accelerate their evolution.

However, to become balanced and begin to polarize properly it is then necessary to investigate movements of all kinds, especially bellicosity.

Kathryn states: "This reminds me of how before the veil of forgetting, typically found more often closer to the center of our galaxy, there wasn't bellicosity due to beings remembering everything and that everyone is a part of the Creator. They also felt that connection to the Creator like an umbilical cord. Due to the happiness and peace, there was less need to serve others so evolution occurred much slower. That's why the veil of forgetting is necessary to polarize faster and therefore eventually move through all the densities."

This third density social memory complex from Sirius investigated bellicosity (war-like mentality) by taking Charlie Hixson on their UFO and extracting from his memory rather than warfare among themselves.

Entities of this heritage would find it nearly impossible to fight. Their studies of movements of all kinds is their form of meditation which must be balanced, just as our people on Earth need constant moments of meditation to balance our activities.

These advanced third density entities from Sirius did not use their legs for movement but of an electromagnetic phenomenon controlled by thought impulses of a weak electrical nature.

Their craft was visible to people on our planet in that area at that time and is a third-density material, like a chair on Earth.

Graduation into fourth-density negative is achieved by those beings who have consciously contacted intelligent infinity through the use of red, orange and yellow rays of energy. Therefore, the planetary conditions of fourth-density negative include the constant alignment and realignment of entities in efforts to form dominant patterns of combined energy.

The early fourth density is one of the most intensive struggles for the negative polarization. When the order of authority has been established and all have fought until convinced that each is in the proper placement for power structure, the social memory complex begins. Always the fourth-density effect of telepathy and the transparency of thought are attempted to be used for the sake of those at the apex of the power structure.

This is often quite damaging to the further polarization of fourth-density negative entities, for the further negative polarization can come about only through group effort. As they manage to combine, they then polarize through such services to self as those offered by the crusaders of Orion.

Session 39: 3-16-1981

Ra: "As you are aware, in the beginning of the creations set up by each Logos, there are created complete potentials, both electrical, in the sense Larson intends, and metaphysical. This metaphysical electricity is important in the understanding of this statement as is the concept of electricity.

This concept deals with potentiated energy. The electron has been said to have no mass but only a field. Others claim a mass of infinitesimal measure. Both are correct. The true mass of the potentiated (more effective or active) energy is the strength of the field. This is also true metaphysically.

However, in your present physical system of knowledge it is useful to take the mass number of the electron in order to do work that you may find solutions to other questions about the physical universe. In such a way, you may conveniently consider each density of being to have a greater and greater spiritual mass. The mass increases significantly but not greatly until the gateway density. In this density the summing up, the looking backwards- in short- all the useful functions of polarity have been used. Therefore, the metaphysical electrical nature of the individual grows greater and greater in spiritual mass.

For an analog one may observe the work of Albert who posits the growing to infinity of mass as this mass approaches the speed of light. Thus, the seventh-density being, the completed being, the Creator who knows Itself, accumulates mass and compacts into the One Creator once again."

$$Mi= \frac{m_0 C^2}{\sqrt{1-v^2/c^2}}$$

Mi in this equation equals spiritual mass. Henry Puharich statement by "The Nine" stated that "CH is a principle which is the revealing principle of knowledge and of law." Ra said that the principle is so veiled in that statement is but the simple principle of the constant or Creator and the transient or the incarnate being and the yearning existing between the two, one for the other, in love and light amidst the distortions of free will acting upon the illusion-bound entity."

"The Nine" transmitted this principle in a veiled way because the scribe is most interested in puzzles and equations.

"The Nine" describes themselves as the "nine principals of God."

This is also a veiled statement. The attempt is made to indicate that the nine who sit upon the Council are those representing the Creator, the One Creator, just as there may be nine witnesses in a courtroom testifying for one defendant. The term principal has this meaning also.

The abilities and preferences of a scribe or contact group determines the nature of this contact. The difference lies in the fact that Ra is as they are, so they will only speak as they are. This demands a very tuned group.

Our development in evolution of the seven bodily energy centers: The basic energy of red ray may be seen to be the basic strengthening ray for each density. It shall never be condescended to less important or productive of spiritual evolution, for it is the foundation ray.

60

The next foundation ray is yellow, the great stepping stone ray. At this ray the mind/body potentiates to its fullest balance. The strong red/orange/yellow triad springboards the entity into the center ray of green. This is a basic ray, but not a primary ray.

Green ray is the resource for spiritual work. When green ray has been activated, we find the third primary ray being able to begin potentiation. This is the first true spiritual ray in that all transfers are of an integrated mind/body/spirit nature.

The blue ray seats the learnings/teachings of the spirit in each density within the mind/body complex animating the whole, communicating to others this entirety of beingness.

The indigo ray, though precious, is only worked upon by the adept. It is the gateway to intelligent infinity bringing intelligent energy through. This is the energy center worked upon in the inner, hidden and occult teachings, for this ray is infinite in its possibilities. Those who heal, teach and work for the Creator in any way may be seen to be both radiant and balanced in those activities that are indigo ray.

The violet ray is constant and is not applied to the functions of ray activation. It is the mark, the register, the identity, the true vibration of the entity.

There is no difference in red ray in equally strongly polarized positive and negative entities.

The negative ray pattern is red/orange/yellow moving directly to the blue. The blue only being used to contact intelligent infinity.

In positively oriented entities the configuration is even, crystal lineally clear of the seven energy rays.

Session 40: 3-18-1981

Our Sun, the sub-Logos, has white light emanating from it made up of frequencies ranging from red to violet.

The white light which emanates and forms articulated sub-Logos has its beginning in what may be metaphysically seen as darkness. The light comes into that darkness and transfigures it, causing the chaos to organize and become reflective or radiant. Thus, the dimensions come into being.

Metaphysically speaking, the blackness of the black hole is a concentration of white light being systematically absorbed once again into the One Creator. Finally, this absorption into the One Creator continues until all the infinity of creations have attained sufficient spiritual mass in order that all form once again the great central sun of the intelligent infinity awaiting potentiation by free will. Thus, the transition of the octave may be seen to enter into timelessness of unimaginable nature moving through the black hole of the ultimate spiritual gravity well and coming immediately into the next octave.

Our astronomers have noticed that light from spiral galaxies is approximately seventy times less than it should be, considering the calculated mass of the galaxy. This is due to the increase of spiritual mass in the galaxy we call white dwarf stars. This is a portion of the way or process of creations cycle.

The first density corresponds to the color red. In first density the red ray is the foundation for all that is to come.

In second density the orange ray is that of movement and growth of the individual, this ray striving towards the yellow ray of self-conscious manifestations of a social and individual nature; third density being the equivalent, and so forth, each density being primarily its ray plus the attractions of the following ray pulling it forward in evolution and to some extent coloring or shading the chief color of that density.

Assuming the individual evolves in a straight line from first through eighth density, the bodily energy centers for an individual would then be activated to completion if everything worked out as it should.

However, the fully activated being is rare. Much emphasis is laid upon the harmonies and balances of individuals. It is necessary for graduation across densities for the primary energy centers to be functioning in such a way as to communicate with intelligent infinity and to appreciate and bask in this light in all of its purity. However, to fully activate each energy center is the mastery of few, for each center has a variable speed of rotation or activity. Once all necessary centers are activated to the minimal necessary degree is the harmony and balance between these energy centers.

Within each density there's a gradual upgrading of vibratory levels.

The frequency of vibration which forms the photon, the core of all particles of the density, increases from a frequency in second density of orange to the third density color of yellow. This transition takes place with the gradual upgrading of vibratory levels within each density.

All the vibrations that form the density, the basic vibrations of the photon, increases in a quantum fashion over a relatively short period of time.

The frequency that is the basis of each density is what may be called a true color. This term is impossible to define given Earth's system of sensibilities and scientific measurements, for color has vibratory characteristics both in space/time and in time/space. The true color is then overlaid and tinged by the rainbow of the various vibratory levels within that density and the attraction vibrations of the next true color density.

The transition from second to third density was approximately 1,350 years.

It's difficult to estimate the transition time from Earth's third density to fourth density due to the uncharacteristic anomalies of this transition. There are incarnate beings who already started fourth density work by the 1980's and most likely before that. However, the third density climate of planetary consciousness is retarding the process.

The possibility/ probability vortices indicate somewhere between 100-700 years as transition period. This could change due to the volatility of people on Earth.

The vibration of the photon has increased in frequency already.

It is this influence that has begun to cause thoughts to become things. As an example, the thoughts of anger becoming cells of the physical body going out of control to become cancer.

This third to fourth density vibratory increase began approximately in 1936 when the first harbingers (forerunners) began their fourth density work. Energies will be vibrating more intensely through the forty-year period preceding the final movement of vibratory matter through the quantum leap.

The vibratory nature of our environment already became true color green before 1981. It was heavily over-woven with the orange ray of planetary consciousness. However, the nature of quanta (or density) is such that the movement over the boundary is that of discrete placement of vibratory level.

The fourth density is one of revealed information. Selves are not hidden to self or other selves. The imbalances or distortions of a destructive nature show, therefore, in more obvious ways, the vehicle of the mind/body/spirit complex thus acting as a teaching resource for self-revelation. These illnesses such as cancer are correspondingly very amenable (agreeable) to self-healing once the mechanism of the destructive influence has been grasped by the individual.

Cancer is quite easily healed mentally and spiritually with fasting and diet used as a link to that healing. Cancer is a good teaching tool because it is easily healed mentally and spiritually with the body used as a link and once the entity forgives the other self who they're angry with and forgive themselves the cancer will disappear.

The other portion of healing has to do with a greatly heightened respect for the self. This may be conveniently expressed by taking care in dietary matters. This is quiet frequently a part of the healing and forgiving process.

These dietary matters for the greatest care of one's body should not be understood literally but as a link or psychological nudge for the body, mind, and spirit. It is the care and respect for the self that is the true thing of importance. Here is the basic information for this instrument's diet, for Carla's diet: The vegetables, the fruits, the grains, and to the extent necessary for the individual metabolism, the animal products. These are those substances showing respect for the self.

In addition, those entities in need of purging the self of a poison thought form or emotion complex do well to take care in following a program of careful fasting until the destructive thought form has been purged analogously (comparable) with the byproducts of ridding the physical body of excess material. The value is not to the body complex but used as a link for the mind and spirit. Thus, self-reveals self to self.

The basic vibration that we experience now is true color green or fourth-density as third density entities. The fourth density vibration we now experience accounts for many mental effects on material such as the bending of metal by mind.

The great number of entities with the so-called mental diseases is due to the effect of this green ray true color upon the mental configurations of those unready mentally to face the self for the first time.

65

People incarnating here by seniority of vibration who have distracted themselves and failed to prepare for this transition are somewhat susceptible to mental diseases or disorders.

Session 41: 3-20-1981

If the (channeling) group moves to another house the place of working for channelings shall be of the appropriate vibratory levels or that purification of the place be enacted and dedication made through mediation before initial working. This might entail such seemingly mundane chores as the cleansing or pointing of surfaces which the group may deem inappropriately marred (flawed).

The banishing Ritual of the Lesser Pentagram can be used in preparing a place for a channeling session.

Our Sun is the sub-Logos that creates all that we experience in our particular solar system.

Ra: "The sun has various aspects in relation to intelligent infinity, to intelligent energy, and to each density of each planet, as you call these spheres. Moreover, these differences extend into the metaphysical or time/space part of your creation.

In relationship to intelligent infinity, the sun body is, equally with all parts of the infinite creation, part of that infinity.

In relationship to the potentiated intelligent infinity which makes use of intelligent energy, it is the offspring of the Logos for a much larger number of sub-Logoi. The relationship is hierarchical in that the sub-Logos uses the intelligent energy in ways set forth by the Logos and uses its free will to co-create the full nuances of your densities as you experience them.

In relationship to the densities, the sun body may physically be seen to be a large body of gaseous elements undergoing the processes of fusion and radiating heat and light."

Metaphysically, the sun achieves a meaning to fourth through seventh density according to the growing abilities of entities in these densities to grasp the living creation and co-entity, or other self, nature of this sun body. Thus, by the sixth density the sun may be visited and inhabited by those dwelling in time/space and may even be partially created from moment to moment by the processes of sixth density entities in their evolution.

Some sixth density entities whose means of reproduction is fusion may choose to perform this portion of experience as part of the beingness of the sun body. You may think of portions of the light that we receive as offspring of the generative expression of sixth-density love. Latter portions of sixth density seeking the experiences of the gateway density are using this mechanism to be more closely Co-Creators with the Infinite Creator.

The sub-Logos is of the entire octave and is not an entity that experiences the learning/teachings of entities such as us humans.

First-density beings is formed by the energy center (vortex). This vortex then causes these spinning motions of vibration of light which then starts to condense into materials of the first density such as water, fire, air and Earth.

The Logos has the plan of all the densities of the octave in potential completion before entering the space/time continuum in first density. Thus, the energy centers exist in potentiation before they are manifest.

The simplest manifest being is light, also known as the photon. In relationship to energy centers, it may be seen to be the center or foundation of all articulated energy fields.

The first or red-ray density, though attracted towards growth, is not in the proper vibration for those conditions conducive (helpful) to the spark of awareness. As the vibratory energies move from red to the vibratory environment that stimulate those chemical substances to combine in such a way that love and light begin the function of growth.

The polymorphous dinoflagellate is a single-celled entity. The mechanism is the attraction of upward spiraling light. There is nothing random about this or any portion of evolution.

The base of any metabolism may be found in the chemical substances of the neighborhood of origin. There are several different types of cell bases for conscious entities on this planet and to a much greater extent in the forms found on other planets of other sub-Logoi (planets in other solar systems.) The chemical vehicle most conveniently houses the consciousness. The functioning of consciousness is more important than the chemical makeup of a physical vehicle.

The polymorphous dinoflagellate has an orange energy center. The true color of orange of second density is precisely the same as the true color of humans being yellow. However, the second-density beginning is primitive and the use of orange ray limited to the expression of self may be seen to be movement and survival.

Those clinging to orange ray in third density have a much more complex system of distortions through which orange ray is manifested.

Ra: "The appropriate true color for third density is yellow. However, the influences of the true color, green, acting upon yellow ray entities have caused many entities to revert to the consideration of self rather than the stepping forward into consideration of other self or green ray. This may not be seen to be of a negatively polarized nature, as the negatively polarized entity is working very intensively with the deepest manifestation of yellow ray group energies, especially the manipulation of other self for service to self. Those reverting to orange ray are many upon your plane at this time, are those who feel the vibrations of true color green and, therefore, respond by rejecting governmental and societal activities as such and seek once more the self.

However, not having developed the yellow ray properly so that it balances the personal vibratory rates of the entity, the entity then is faced with the task of further activation and balancing of the self, thus the orange ray manifestations at this space/time nexus.

Thus, true color orange is without difference. However, the manifestations of this or any ray may be seen to be most various depending upon the vibratory levels and balances of the mind/body/spirit complexes which are expressing these energies."

Our scientists have puzzled over the various differences and possible interrelationships of various stages, types, and conditions of life forms. This is not fruitful information as the Sun (Sub-Logos) in a moment's choice can change it if it chooses.

Animals and those of a vegetable nature, like a tree, are the first to experience yellow ray experiences that find the necessity for reproduction by bisexual techniques or who find it necessary to depend in some way on other selves for survival and growth.

Each energy center may potentially be activated in third density, the late second-density entities having the capability, if efficient use is made of experience, of vibrating and activating the green ray energy center.

The third-density being, having the potential for complete self-awareness, thus has the potential for the minimal activation of all energy centers. The fourth, fifth, and sixth densities are those refining the higher energy centers. The seventh density is a density of completion and the turning towards timelessness or foreverness.

A second density animal has all of the energy centers but just not all activated. Animals are composed of light just as all things are.

The will of the Logos posits the potentials available to the evolving entity. The will of the entity as it evolves is the single measure of the rate and fastidiousness (very attentive to detail) of the activation and balancing of the various energy centers.

Each energy center has a wide range of rotational speed or people may see it more clearly in relation to color, brilliance (intense brightness of light or vividness of color). The more strongly the will of the entity concentrates upon and refines or purifies each energy center, the more brilliant or rotationally active each energy center will be. It is not necessary for the energy centers to be activated in order for the self-aware entity. Thusly, entities may have extremely brilliant energy centers while being quite unbalanced in their violet ray aspect due to lack of attention paid to the totality of experience of the entity.

The key to balance may be seen in the unstudied, spontaneous, and honest response of entities toward experiences, thus using experience to the utmost, then applying the balancing exercises and achieving the proper attitude for the purified spectrum of energy center manifestation in violet ray. This is why the brilliance or rotational speed of the energy centers is not more important than the balanced violet ray manifestation of an entity in regarding harvestability. Those entities that are unbalanced, especially to the primary rays, will not be capable of sustaining the impact of the love and light of intelligent infinity to the extent necessary for harvest.

Space/time in mathematical terms as Larson uses is s/1. Space being invisible and metaphysical.

Time/space in mathematical terms is t/s. Time being visible third density earth and the physical aspects we see in our dimension.

Fasting to remove unwanted thought forms is a healing technique used by a conscious being. One must be conscious that the ridding of excess and unwanted material from the body is the analogy to the riding of mind or spirit of excess or unwanted material. So, the denial of the unwanted portion is taken through

70

the tree of mind down through the trunk to subconscious levels where the connection is made and the mind, body, spirit in unison expresses denial of the excess or unwanted spiritual or mental material as part of the entity.

All then falls away and the entity, while understanding and appreciating the nature of the rejected material as part of the greater self. Nevertheless, through the action of the will purifies and refines the mind/body/spirit complex, brining into manifestation the desired mind or spirit complex attitude.

Some entities catalyst is programmed by the Higher Self to create experiences so that they can release themselves from unwanted biases. The entity then can consciously program this release through fasting. The self, if conscious to a great enough extent of the working of this catalyst and the techniques of programming, may through concentration of the will and faith alone cause reprogramming without the analogy of fasting, diet or other analogous body complex disciplines.

The material in INITIATION has Ra's teachings on balancing with distortions seen when that material is collated (combined to create a set) with the material Ra has given in the Law of One books.

Red, yellow and blue are the primary energy centers. These are the first, third and fifth rays. They are primary because they signify activity of a primary nature.

Red ray is the foundation;

Orange ray is the movement towards yellow ray.

Yellow is self-awareness and interaction.

Green is the movement through various experiences of energy exchanges having to do with compassion and all-forgiving love to the primary blue ray.

Blue is the first ray of radiation of self regardless of any actions from another.

Green-ray entity is ineffectual (ineffective) in the face of blockage from other selves. The blue ray entity is co-Creator. The function of the Logos is a representative of the Infinite Creator in effectuating (putting into operation) the knowing of the Creator by the Creator you may see the steps by which this may be accomplished.

Ra experienced the vibratory densities upon Venus. They were fortunate in being able to move in harmony with the planetary vibrations with a harmonious graduation to second, third, and to fourth, and a greatly accelerated fourth-density experience.

Ra spent much time/space in fifth density balancing the intense compassion they had gained in fourth density. The graduation again was harmonious and their social memory complex had become most firmly cemented in fourth density remained of a very strong and helpful nature.

Their sixth-density work was also accelerated because of harmony of their social memory complex so that they were able to set out as members of the Confederation to even more swiftly approach graduation to seventh density. Their harmony, however, has been a grievous source of naivete as regards to working with Earth entities.

Session 42: 3-22-1981

Someone first experiencing feelings and then consciously discovering their antitheses (the opposite feeling) within the being doesn't have a smooth flow of positive and negative feelings while remaining unswayed but rather the goal of becoming unswayed. This is a simpler result and takes much practice. Therefore, a balanced entity would have the objective of becoming unswayed or unemotional in any given situation.

The catalyst of experience works in order for the learn/teachings of this density to occur. However, if there is seen in a being a response, even if it is simply observed, the entity is still using the catalyst for learn/teaching. The end result is that the catalyst is no longer needed. This is not indifference or objectivity but a finely tuned compassion and love which sees all things as love. This seeing elicits (draws out) no response due to catalytic reactions. Thus, this entity is now able to become co-Creator of experiential occurrences. This is the truer balance.

A perfectly balanced entity when attacked by the other self, such as a bull or a third density being, the response would be love. However, the balanced entity will see the attack from a third density being of a more complex nature than the cause of the attack from the second-density bull. This balanced entity would be open to many more opportunities for service to a third-density other self.

An attack causing physical pain or loss of life would maintain a response of love in a balanced entity as they see the other self who attacked them as the Creator and loving both and understanding their action in attacking you.

Kathryn says: "Every being is learning and operating in their state of awareness and understanding."

Book 2 Continues: This is of a major or principal importance in understanding the principle of balance. Balance is not indifference but rather the observer not blinded by any feelings of separation but rather fully imbued (permeated) with love.

The fourth density abounds in compassion. This compassion if folly when seen through the eyes of fifth density wisdom. The fourth density compassion is the salvation of third density but creates a mismatch in the ultimate balance of an entity.

Thus Ra, as a social memory complex of fourth density, had the tendency towards compassion even to martyrdom in aid of other selves. When the fifth-density harvest was achieved they found in this vibratory level flaws of such unrelieved compassion. They spent much time/space in contemplation of those ways of the Creator which imbue (saturates) love with wisdom in 5th density.

Many third density entities on Earth feel great compassion for relieving the physical problems of third-density other selves by giving them food if there is hunger. Ra says this is the appropriate response. Many people also bring medicine if they feel there is a need to minister to them medically, and being selfless in all of these services to a very great extent.

Starving entities experience catalysts for third density. Giving people food and medicine is creating a vibration in harmony with green ray fourth density. It is the free will of an entity to give food and medicine to others who need it as it is an appropriate response within the framework of our third density learn/teaching at this time which involves the growing sense of love for and service to other selves.

However, the green ray response is not as refined as imbued with wisdom. This wisdom enables the entity to appreciate its contributions to the planetary consciousness by the quality of its being without regard to activities or behaviors expecting results upon visible planes. The balance with this act of love combined with wisdom could be giving them knowledge of the Law of one and the information necessary to reach the state of awareness of fourth density compassion and all-forgiving love.

With the truly balanced entity no situation would be emotionally charged.

The repression of emotions depolarizes the entity in so far as it chooses not to use the catalytic action of the space/time present in a spontaneous manner, thus dimming the energy centers. There is some polarization towards positive if the cause of the repression is consideration for other selves. The entity that worked long enough with the catalyst to be able to feel the catalyst but not find it necessary to express reactions is not yet balanced but suffers no depolarization due to the transparency of its experiential continuum. Thus, the gradual increase in the ability to observe one's reaction and to know the self will bring the self ever closer to a true balance. Patience is requested and suggested, for the catalyst is intense on Earth and its use must be appreciated over a period of consistent learn/teaching.

To a balanced entity no situation has an emotional charge but is simply a situation like any other in which an entity may or may not observe an opportunity to be of service. The closer an entity comes to this attitude the closer an entity is to balance. Reactions to catalyst shouldn't be repressed or suppressed unless such reactions would be a stumbling block not consonant with the Law of One to an other-self. It is far, far better to allow the experience to express itself in order that the entity may then make fuller use of this catalyst.

The thoughts of an entity, its feelings or emotions, and least of all its behavior are the signposts for teaching of self by self. In the analysis of one's experiences of a dinurnal cycle (a day) an entity may assess what it considers to be inappropriate thoughts, behaviors, feelings, and emotions.

In examining these inappropriate activities of mind, body, and spirit complexes the entity may then place these distortions in the proper vibrational ray and see where work is needed.

When the self is conscious to a great enough extent of the workings of catalyst of fasting through concentration of the will by wishing to extend the attention span and hold it upon the desired programming. This, when continued, strengthens the will. The entire activity can only occur when there exists faith that an outcome of this discipline is possible to cause reprogramming without the analogy of fasting, diet or other analogous (comparable) bodily complex disciplines.

Focusing of the attention is the one technique the higher self uses to grow the will and faith to ensure that the desired lessons are learned or attempted by the third-density self.

Many mystical traditions of our people of Earth have common exercises for helping to increase the attention span. The visualization of a shape and color of personal inspirational quality to the mediator is the heart of the religious aspects of this sort of visualization.

The visualization of simple shapes and colors that have no inspirational quality to the entity form the basis for Earth's magical traditions.

Whether someone visualizes the rose or a circle is not important. However, a path towards visualization be chosen in order to exercise expanding the attention span. This is due to the careful arrangement of shapes and colors which have been described as visualizations by those steeped in the magical tradition.

A less sensitized individual is suggested to choose a personally inspirational image. Whether it be the rose which is of perfect beauty, the cross which is perfect sacrifice, the Buddha which is the All-being in One, or whatever else may inspire the individual.

The appropriate teach/learning device of parent to child is the open-hearted beingness of the parent and the total acceptance of the beingness of the child. This will encompass whatever material the child entity has brought into the life experience on this Earth.

There are two things especially important in this relationship other than the basic acceptance of the child by the parent. Firstly, the experience of whatever means the parent uses to worship and give thanksgiving to the One Infinite Creator, should if possible be shared with the child entity upon a daily basis. Secondly, the compassion of parent to child with the understanding that the child entity shall learn the biases of service-to-others or service-to-self from the parental other self. This is the reason that some discipline is appropriate in the teach/learning. This does not activate any energy center for each entity is unique and each relationship with self and other self doubly unique. The guidelines given are only general for this reason.

Session 43: 3-24-1981

Parts removed from cattle mutilations are the same every time. This is related to energy centers, as there is a link between energy centers and various thought forms. Thus, the fears of mass consciousness create the climate for the concentration upon the removal of bodily parts which symbolize areas of concern or fear in the mass consciousness.

The parts removed are related to the mass consciousness fear of third-density humans. The thought form entities feed upon fear from the Orion's and are able to do precise damage according to systems of symbology. The other second-density types need the blood and are creatures of the Orion group. They do not exist in astral planes as the thought forms but wait within the Earth's surface. Ra's impression is that this information is unimportant but the questioner Don Elkins asked, so Ra answered.

When the Creator's light is split or divided into colors and energy centers for experience, in order to reunite with the Creator, the energy centers must be relatively balanced the same as the split light was as it originated from the Creator as opposed to the relative unimportance of maximal activation of each energy center.

Thus, the most fragile entity may be more balanced than one with extreme energy and activity in service-to-others due to the fastidiousness (extreme attention to detail) that the will is focused upon the use of experience in knowing the self. The densities beyond third give the minimally balanced individual much time/space and space/time to continue to refine these inner balances.

Kathryn states: "I spent the first 25 years of my life having all the experiences in the world; traveling, BMX racing from eight years old to 25 years old, sports, scooters, no TV, riding around the neighborhood. Then, I broke my neck to be forced to go inside myself more, which led me to all this research. I was constantly learning as much as I could and I eventually found the truth that resonated with my inner heart such as the Law of One. Now I balance both service-to-others through giving humanity this information and truth to help more people make the fourth density harvest. This immense dedication is also balanced with taking a day or two off a week for a show, movie, working out, sleeping in and exploring the outside world; just having fun."

The use of physical pain is minimal in fourth density, having only to do with the end of the fourth-density incarnation. This physical pain would not be considered severe enough to treat in third density. The catalysts of mental and spiritual pain are used in fourth density.

The variety of pain of weariness is a part of physical pain at the end of fourth density.

The space/time incarnation of harmonious fourth density experience is approximately 90,000 years. There are multiple incarnations in fourth density with time/space experiences in between incarnations.

The cycle of experience is approximately 30 million years (for fourth density) if the entities are not capable of being harvested sooner. There is in this density a harvest which is completely the readiness of the social memory complex. It is not structured like third density, for it deals with a more transparent distortion of the One Infinite Creator.

At the end of third density the individual is harvested as a function of violet ray, but the violet ray of the entire social memory complex for fourth density must vibrate at the appropriate level to graduate to fifth density.

In fifth density entities may choose to learn as a social memory complex or as a mind/body/spirit complexes and may graduate to sixth density individually or as a social memory complex. For the wisdom density is an extremely free density whereas the lessons of compassion leading to wisdom have to do with other selves.

Sixth-density harvest is of a social memory complex graduation because we have wisdom and compassion blended back using wisdom.

The chemical elements of a fourth-density physical body are not the same as a third-density body. However, the appearance is similar.

It is necessary to eat food in fourth density. The fourth-density being desires to serve and the preparation of food is extremely simple due to increased communion between entity and living foodstuff. Therefore, this is not a significant catalyst but a simple precondition of the space/time experience. This is not considered to be of importance by fourth-density entities and it, therefore, aids in the teach/learning of patience. To stop the functioning of service-to-others long enough to ingest food is to invoke patience.

Fifth-density entities need food which may be prepared by thought. They would eat nectar or ambrosia, or a light broth of golden white hue. Ingesting food in fifth-density is a somewhat central point. The purpose of space/time is the increase in catalytic action appropriate to the density. One of the preconditions for space/time existence is some form of body complex. Such as a body complex fueled in some way.

Fueling our body in third density not only fuels our body that we need but gives us opportunity to learn service and patience. In fifth density it fuels the body and becomes a solace (comfort or relief) rather than a catalyst for learning. In fifth density it is a comfort for those of like-minded gathered together to share in this broth, thus becoming one in light and wisdom while joining hearts and hands in physical activity.

Food in sixth density is light.

The probability/possibility vortices indicate that after the harvest is complete on Earth, there most likely will be incarnate fourth-density beings on the surface as third density entities are now. There won't be any fifth or sixth-density beings on Earth for a long time as fourth-density beings need to spend their learn/teaching space/time with their own density's entities.

As fourth-density beings progress they have more and more need for other density teachings like the information Ra gives due to the calling, so the information is always available. Fifth-density beings just won't live on the surface of the planet until the planet reaches fifth-density vibratory level.

Experience in fourth density is emphatically (without doubt) not the same as third-density experience. It is necessary first for a call to exist for the teach/learning of fifth density to be given to fourth just as a calling in third-density predisposes the information received in a way consonant with free will.

Ra previously stated that the key to strengthening the will is concentration.

An isolation-type of situation is one of the functions of the pyramid.

Free will may be focused at any object or goal.

Without infringing upon free will Ra feels it is possible to state that the Faraday cage and the isolation tank are gadgets in mediation to avoid some distractions as the channeling group asked for this information.

The surrounding of self in a sylvan atmosphere (woods), apart from distractions, in a place of working used for no other purpose, in which the questioner and his associates agree to lay aside all goals but that of the meditative seeking of the Infinite Creator is not gadgetry but the making use of the creation of the Father in second-density love, and in love and support of other selves.

Session 46: 4-15-1981

Kathryn says: "Session 44 and 45 were removed from the channeling group. My notes from those sessions in book 5 will be at the end of that book from those two sessions."

An entity polarizing positively perceives anger instead of using anger for control.

Ra: "The entity polarizing positively perceives the anger. This entity, if using this catalyst mentally, blesses and loves this anger in itself. It then intensifies this anger consciously in mind alone until the folly of this red-ray energy is perceived not as folly in itself but as energy subject to spiritual entropy due to the randomness of energy being used.

Positive orientation then provides the will and faith to continue this mentally intense experience of letting the anger be understood, accepted, and integrated with the mind/body/spirit complex. The other self which is the object of anger is thus transformed into an object of acceptance, understanding, and accommodation, all being reintegrated using the great energy which anger began.

The negatively oriented mind/body/spirit complex will use this anger in a similarly conscious fashion, refusing to accept the undirected or random energy of anger and instead, through will and faith, funneling this energy into a practical means of venting the negative aspect of this emotion so as to obtain control over other self, or otherwise control the situation causing anger.

Control is the key to negatively polarized use of catalyst. Acceptance is the key to positively polarized use of catalyst. Between these polarities lies the potential for this random and undirected energy creating a bodily complex analog (similar) of what you call the cancerous growth of tissue."

The first acceptance, or control depending upon polarity, is of self. Anger is one of many things to be accepted and loved as part of self or controlled as a part of self, if the entity is to do work.

If a negatively polarizing entity is unable to control his own anger or unable to control himself in anger, he may cause cancer. The negative polarization contains a great requirement for control and repression.

Any mind complex distortion that's emotional and disorganized needs, in order to be useful to the negatively oriented entity, to be repressed and then brought to the surface in an organized use. You may find for instance, negatively polarized entities controlling and repressing such basic bodily complex needs as the sexual desire in order that in the practice the will may be used to enforce itself upon the other self with greater efficiency when the sexual behavior is allowed.

A positively oriented entity, rather than attempting repression of emotion, would balance the emotion such as the acceptance and love of anger as part of self as previously stated. This illustrates the path of unity.

Catalyst is unconscious and does not work with intelligence. It is a part of the learn/teaching set up by the sub-Logos before the beginning of our space/time.

In many cases catalyst is not used when the entity developing cancer has no conscious idea of what is happening to them when they develop cancer.

The catalyst, and all catalyst, is designed to offer experience. This experience in our density may be loved and accepted or it may be controlled. These are two paths. When neither path is chosen the catalyst fails in its design and the entity proceeds until catalyst strikes again causing it to form a bias towards acceptance and love or separation and control. There is no lack of space/time in which this catalyst may work.

After Ra stated that the instrument (Carla) grows weary, Ra indicated the possibility of two sessions per week to not cause further harm to the instrument of low physical energy and the potential of the psychic attacks from negative entities not wanting this truth to get out to the world that would raise the consciousness of the planet and interfere with their negatively polarized agenda. (The attacks were from fourth and fifth density negative Orion entities or demons attacking Wanderers so that this information doesn't get out.) Ra appreciates the channeling groups fidelity (the faithfulness) and commitment to this process for their service to humanity.

Session 47: 4-18-1981

The social memory complexes were not planned by the Logos or sub-Logos. As the unity of the Creator exists within the smallest portion of any material created by Love, much less is a self-aware being.

However, the distortion of free will causes the social memory complex to appear as a possibility at a certain stage of evolution of mind. The purpose, or consideration that causes entities to form complexes, of these social memory complexes, is a very simple extension of the basic distortion towards the Creator's knowing of Itself, for when a group of mind/body/spirits becomes able to form a social memory complex, all experience of each entity is available to the whole of the complex. Thus, the Creator knows more of Its creation in each entity partaking of this communion of entities.

The vibratory rates are not the same in positive and negative orientation. They have the power to accept and work with intelligent infinity to a certain degree or intensity. Due to the fact that the primary color of blue energy is missing from the negatively-oriented system of power, the green/blue vibratory energies are not seen in the fourth and fifth density negative vibrations.

The positive has the full spectrum of true color time/space vibratory patterns and thus contains a variant vibratory pattern.

Each is capable of doing fourth-density work. This is criterion for harvest.

All beings have the potential for all possible vibratory rates. The potential of green and blue center activation is precisely where it must be in a creation of Love. However, the negatively polarized entity will have achieved harvest due to extremely efficient use of red and yellow/orange, moving directly to the gateway indigo bringing through this intelligent energy channel the insteamings of intelligent infinity.

The positive/negative polarity at the sixth level (sixth density) simply becomes history. Therefore, Ra speaks in an illusory time continuum discussing statistics of positive versus negative harvest into fifth. A large percentage of fourth-density experience, for without wisdom the compassion and desire to aid other self is not extremely well informed.

Visual aids or training aids available in fourth density automatically aids the entity in polarization while extremely cutting down upon the quick effect of catalyst. Therefore, fourth density must take up more space/time.

The percentage of positively oriented entities will harmoniously approach 98% in intention. The primary qualification for graduation from fourth to fifth density is understanding. To achieve this graduation the entity must be able to understand the actions, the movements, and the dance. It is a measure of efficiency of perception. It may be measured by light. The ability to love, accept and use a certain intensity of light creates the requirement for both positive and negative fourth to fifth density harvesting.

When a crystalline structure is formed of Earth's physical material the elements present in each molecule are bonded in a regularized fashion with elements in each other molecule. The structure is regular and has certain properties when fully and perfectly crystallized. It will not splinter or break; it is very strong without effort; and it is radiant, traducing (misrepresenting) light into a beautiful refraction giving pleasure to the eye of many.

There are numerous bodies listed in esoteric literature.

Ra: "For the interrelationships of the various bodies and each body's effects in various situations is an enormous study. However, we shall begin by referring your minds back to the spectrum of true colors and the usage of this understanding in grasping the various densities of your octave.

We have the number seven repeated from the macrocosm (universe) to the microcosm (universe encapsulating a miniature version such as humankind) in structure and experience. Therefore, it would only be expected that there would be seven basic bodies which we would perhaps be most lucid (easily understood) by stating as red-ray body, ect. However, we are aware that you wish to correspond these bodies mentioned with the color rays... Various teachers have offered their teach/learning understanding in various terms. Thus, one may name a subtle body one thing and another find a different name.

The red-ray body is your chemical body. However, it is not the body which you have as clothing in the physical. It is the unconstructed material of the body, the elemental body without form. This basic unformed material body is important to understand for there are healings which may be carried out by the simple understanding of the elements present in the physical vehicle.

The orange-ray body is the physical body complex. This body complex is still not the body you inhabit but rather the body formed without self-awareness, the body in the womb before the spirit/mind complex enters. This body may live without the inhabitation of the mind and spirit complexes. However, it seldom does so.

The yellow-ray body is your physical vehicle which you know of at this time and in which you experience catalyst. This body has the mind/body/spirit characteristics and is equal to the physical illusion.

The green-ray body is that body which may be seen in séance (a spiritualist who can communicate with spirits) when what you call ectoplasm (supernatural substance, which may appear as white) is furnished. This is a lighter body packed more densely with life. You may call this the astral body following some other teachings. Others have called this same body the etheric body. However, this is not correct in the sense that the etheric body is that body of gateway wherein intelligent energy is able to mold the mind/body/spirit complex.

The light body or blue-ray body may be called the devachanic (non-physical) body. There are many other names for this body especially in your so-called Indian Sutras or writings, for there are those among these peoples which have explored these regions and understand the various types of devachanic bodies. There are many, many types of bodies in each density, much like your own.

The indigo-ray body which we (Ra) choose to call the etheric body is, the gateway body. In this body form is substance and you may only see this body as light as it may mold itself as it desires.

The violet-ray body may perhaps be understood as what you might call the Buddha body or that body which is complete.

Each of these bodies has an effect upon your mind/body/spirit complex in your life beingness. The interrelationships are many and complex.

Perhaps one suggestion that may be indicated is this: the indigo-ray body may be used by the healer once the healer becomes able to place its consciousness in this etheric state. The violet-ray or Buddhic body is of equal efficacy (power to produce a desired result) to the healer for within it lies a sense of wholeness which is extremely close to unity with all that there is. These bodies are part of each entity and the proper use of them and understanding of them is, though far advanced from the standpoint of third-density harvest, nevertheless useful to the adept."

We all have bodies in potentiation.

In our present third density incarnation the yellow-ray body is not in potentiation but in activation, it being that body that is manifest.

The first body which activates itself upon death is the "form-maker" indigo-ray body. This body remains the "ka" until ethereal has been penetrated and understanding has been gained by the mind/body/spirit totality. Once this is achieved, if the proper body to be activated is green ray, then this will occur.

After death, if an entity is unaware, he may become an Earth-bound spirit or lingering ghost until he is able to achieve the required awareness for activation of one of his bodies.

The will would create the Earth-bound spirit or a lingering ghost. If the will of the yellow-ray mind/body/spirit is stronger than the progressive impetus (driving force) of the physical death towards realization of what comes next. That is, if the will is concentrative enough on the previous experience, the entity's yellow ray shell, though no longer activated, cannot be completely deactivated until the will is released and the mind/body/spirit complex is caught. This often occurs in sudden death and in the case of extreme concern for a thing or an other-self.

Orange-ray activation after death on Earth occurs quite infrequently, due to the fact that this particular manifestation is without will. Occasionally, someone else will demand the form of the one passing that some semblance (outward appearance) of the being will remain. This is orange ray. This is rare, for normally if one entity desires another enough to call it, the entity will have the corresponding desire to be called, that manifestation would be yellow ray.

The normal procedure, given a harmonious passage of death from yellow ray manifestation, is for the mind and spirit complex to rest in the etheric (indigo ray) body until the entity begins its preparation for experience in an incarnated place that has a manifestation formed by the etheric energy molding it into activation and manifestation. This indigo body, being intelligent energy, is able to offer the newly dead soul a perspective and place to view the experience most recently manifested.

Session 48: 4-22-1981

Ra believes it is more effective to send love/light to our peoples on Earth and the treasure of this contact with the group (Carla, Don, and Jim) than to be naïve enough again to think their physical presence would be more effective. If Ra were to walk the Earth, they would offer themselves as teach/learners.

Orion entities cause UFO flaps by visibly appearing in our skies. The flaps cause many fears among people on Earth, many speaking's, understandings concerning plots, cover-ups, mutilations, killings, and other negative impressions. Even those supposedly positive reports which gain public awareness speak of doom. The understandings in this book are part of the minority.

The Orion-type UFO publicity brought an audience not seeded (planted) by seniority of vibration to a great extent. (Those in fear had less Law of One awareness and a lower vibration.) The audiences receiving teach/learnings without stimulus of fear from publicity will be more greatly oriented towards illumination (awareness and enlightenment).

Ra: "I am Ra. There is very little work in consciousness in fourth and in fifth densities compared to the work done in third density. The work that is accomplished in positive fourth is work whereby the positive social memory complex, having, through slow stages, harmoniously integrated itself, goes forth to aid those of less positive orientation which seek their aid. Thus, their service is their work and through this dynamic between the societal self and the other self, which is the object of love, greater and greater intensities of understanding or compassion are attained. This intensity continues until the appropriate intensity of the light may be welcomed. This is fourth-density harvest.

Within fourth-density positive there are minor amounts of catalyst of a spiritual and mental complex distortion. This occurs during the process of harmonizing to the extent of forming the social memory complex. This causes some small catalyst and work to occur, but the great work of fourth density lies in the contact betwixt the societal self and less polarized other self.

In fourth-density negative much work is accomplished during the fighting for position which precedes the period of the social memory complex. There are opportunities to polarize negatively by control of other selves. During the social memory complex period of fourth-density negative the situation is the same. The work takes place through the societal reaching out to less polarized other self in order to aid in negative polarization.

In fifth-density positive and negative the concept of work done through a potential difference is not particularly helpful as fifth-density entities are, again, intensifying rather than potentiating.

In positive, the fifth-density complex uses sixth-density teach/learners to study the more illuminated (enlightening) understandings of unity thus becoming more and more wise. Fifth-density positive social memory complexes will choose to divide their service to others in two ways: first, the beaming of light to creation; second, the sending of groups to be of aid as instruments of light such as those whom you are familiar with through channels.

In fifth-density negative, service to self has become extremely intense and the self has shrunk or compacted so that the dialogues with the teach/learners are used exclusively in order to intensify wisdom. There are very, very few fifth-density negative Wanderers for the fear of the forgetting. There are very, very few fifth-density Orion members for they do not any longer perceive any virtue (worthiness) in other selves."

Each mind/body/spirit complex has its own patterns of activation and its own rhythms of awakening. The important thing for harvest is the harmonious balance between the various energy centers of the mind/body/spirit complex. This is of relative importance."

Each creation is not alike. Each mind/body/spirit complex has its own patterns of activation and its own rhythms of awakening. The important thing for harvest is the harmonious balance between the various energy centers of the mind/body/spirit complex. This is to be noted of relative importance.

Ra: "The entity, before incarnation, dwells in the appropriate place in time/space. The true color types of this location will be dependent upon the entity's needs. Wanderers, have the green, blue, or indigo true color core of mind/body/spirit complex will have rested therein.

Entrance into incarnation requires the investment or activation of the indigo ray or etheric body for this is the "form-maker." The young or small physical mind/body/spirit complex has the seven energy centers potentiated before the birthing process. There are also analogs (devices of information) in time/space of these energy centers in each of the seven true color densities. Thus, in the microcosm (universe) exists all the experience that is prepared. It is as though the infant contains the universe.

The patterns of activation of an entity of high seniority will undoubtedly move with some rapidity to the green-ray level which is the springboard to primary blue. There is always some difficulty in penetrating blue primary energy for it requires that which your people have in great paucity (deficiency); that is, honesty. Blue ray is the ray of free communication with self and with other self. Having accepted that an harvestable or nearly harvestable entity will be working from this green-ray springboard one may then posit that the experiences in the remainder of the incarnation will be focused upon activation of the primary blue ray of freely given communication, of indigo ray, that of freely shared intelligent energy, and if possible, moving through this gateway, the penetration of violet-ray intelligent infinity. This may be seen to be manifested by a sense of the consecrate (sacred) of hallowed (holy) nature of everyday creations and activities.

Upon the bodily complex death, the entity will immediately, upon realization of its state, return to the indigo form-maker body and rest therein until the proper future placement is made.

Here we have the anomaly (abnormal) of harvest. In harvest the entity will then transfer its indigo body into violet-ray manifestation as seen in true color yellow. This is for the purpose of gauging the harvestability of the entity. After this anomalous (abnormal) activity has been carefully completed, the entity will move into indigo body again and be placed in the correct true color locus (location) in space/time and time/space at which time the healings and learn/teachings necessary shall be completed and further incarnation needs determined."

Those under the Guardians are responsible for the determination of further incarnation needs of those incarnating automatically without conscious self-awareness of the process of spiritual evolution. They have been referred to as angelic beings. They are "local" or of our planetary sphere.

Ra: "The seniority of vibration is to be likened unto placing various grades of liquids in the same glass. Some will rise to the top; others will sink to the bottom. Layers and layers of entities will ensue. As harvest draws near, those filled with the most light and love will naturally, and without supervision, be in line for the experience of incarnation.

When the entity becomes aware in its mind/body/spirit complex totality of the mechanism for spiritual evolution it, itself, will arrange and place those lessons and entities necessary for maximum growth and expression of polarity in the incarnative experience before the forgetting process occurs. The only disadvantage of this total free will of those senior entities choosing the manner of incarnation experiences is that some entities attempt to learn so much during one incarnative experience that the intensity of catalyst disarranges the polarized entity and the experience is not maximally useful as intended."

An analogy (resemblance) to that would be a student in college signing up for more courses than he could possibly assimilate (absorb) in the time given.

Each of the true color densities has the seven energy centers and each entity contains all this in potentiation. The activation, while in yellow ray, of violet-ray intelligent infinity is a passport to the next octave of experience. There are adepts (beings who have freed themselves from the thoughts and opinions of others) who have penetrated many, many of the energy centers and several of the true colors. This must be done in the utmost care while in the physical body for there are dangers linking red/orange/yellow circuitry with true color blue circuitry the potential for disarrangement of the mind/body/spirit complex is great. However, the entity who penetrates intelligent infinity is basically capable of walking the universe with unfettered (unrestrained) treat.

Session 49: 4-27-1981

The lobes of our physical complex brain are alike in their use of weak electrical energy. The entity ruled by intuition and impulse is equal to the entity governed by rational analysis when polarity is considered.

Ra: "The lobes may both be used for service to self or service-to-others. It may seem that the rational or analytical mind might have more of a possibility of successfully pursuing the negative orientation due to the fact that in our understanding too much order is by its essence negative. However, this same ability to structure abstract concepts and to analyze experiential data may be the key to rapid positive polarization. It may be said that those whose analytical capacities are predominant have somewhat more to work with in polarizing.

The function of intuition is to inform intelligence. In your illusion the unbridled (uncontrolled) predominance (domination) of intuition will tend to keep an entity from the greater polarizations due to the vagaries (unpredictability) of intuitive perception. These two types of brain structures need to be balanced in order that the net sum of experiential catalyst will be polarization and illumination, for without the acceptance by the rational mind of the worth of the intuitive faculty of the creative aspects which aid in illumination (enlightenment) will be stifled (dimmed).

There is one correspondence between right and left and positive and negative. The web of energy which surrounds your bodies contains somewhat complex polarizations. The left area of the head and upper shoulder is most generally seen to be of a negative polarization whereas the right is of positive polarization, magnetically speaking. This is the cause of the tones." (The meaning of the ringing in our ears.)

There is a correlation between the energy field of an entity of our nature and planetary bodies, for all material is constructed by means of the dynamic tension of the magnetic field.

Ra: "The lines of force in both cases may be seen to be much like the interweaving spirals of the braided hair. Thus, positive and negative wind interweave forming geometric relationships in the energy fields of both persons and planets.

The negative pole is the south pole or the lower pole. The north or upper pole is positive. The crisscrossing of these spiraling energies form primary, secondary, and tertiary energy centers. You are familiar with the primary energy centers of the physical, mental, and spiritual body complex. Secondary points of the crisscrossing of positive and negative center orientation revolve about several of your centers. The yellow-ray center may be seen to have secondary energy centers in elbow, in knee, and in the subtle bodies at a slight spacing from the physical vehicle at points describing diamonds about the entity's naval area surrounding the body.

One may examine each of the energy centers for secondary centers. Some of your peoples work with these energy centers, and call this acupuncture. However, it is to be noted that there are most often anomalies (abnormalities) in the placement of the energy centers so that the scientific precision (accuracy) of this practice is brought into question. Like most scientific attempts at precision, it fails to take into account the unique qualities of each creation.

The most important concept to grasp about the energy field is that the lower or negative pole will draw the universal energy into itself from the cosmos. Therefrom, it will move upward to be met and reacted to by the positive spiraling energy moving downward from within. The measure of an entity's level of ray activity is the locus (location) wherein the south pole outer energy has been met by the inner spiraling positive energy.

As an entity grows more polarized this locus will move upwards. This phenomenon has been called by your peoples the kundalini. However, it may be thought of as the meeting place of cosmic and inner vibratory understanding. To attempt to raise the locus (location) of this meeting without realizing the metaphysical principles of magnetism upon which this depends is to invite great imbalance."

Ra: "I am Ra. The metaphor of the coiled serpent being called upwards is vastly appropriate for consideration by your peoples. This is what you are attempting when you seek. There are great misapprehensions (misinterpretations) concerning this metaphor and the nature of pursuing its goal. We must generalize and ask that you grasp the fact that this in effect renders far less useful what we share. However, as each entity is unique, generalities are our lot when communicating for your possible edification (benefit)."

Ra: "We have two types of energy. We are attempting then, as entities in any true color of this octave, to move the meeting place of inner and outer natures further and further along or upward along the energy centers. The two methods of approaching this with sensible (easily affected) methods are first,

94

the seating within one's self of those experiences which are attracted to the entity through the south pole. Each experience will need to be observed, experienced, balanced, accepted, and seated within the individual. As the entity grows in self-acceptance and awareness of catalyst the location of the comfortable seating of these experiences will rise to the new true color entity. The experience, whatever it may be, will be seated in red ray and considered as to its survival content and so forth.

Each experience will be sequentially (following a logical order) and understood by the growing and seeking mind/body/spirit complex in terms of survival, then in terms of personal identity, then in terms of social relation, then in terms of universal love, then in terms of how the experience may beget (bring) free communication, then in terms of how the experience may be linked to universal energies, and finally in terms of the sacramental nature (sacred signs) of each experience.

Meanwhile the Creator lies within. In the north pole the crown is already upon the head and the entity is potentially a god. This energy is brought into being by the humble and trusting acceptance of this energy through meditation and contemplation of the self and of the Creator.

Where these energies meet is where the serpent will have achieved its height. When this uncoiled energy approaches universal love and radiant being the entity is in a state whereby the harvestability of the entity comes nigh."

Leaving the mind as blank as possible in meditation and letting it run down, so to speak, or focusing on some object or something for concentration is another way to meditate.

Ra: "Each of the two types of meditation is useful for a particular reason. The passive meditation involving the clearing of the mind, the emptying of the mental jumble which is characteristic of mind complex activity among your peoples, is efficacious (effective) for those whose goal is to achieve an inner silence as a base from which to listen to the Creator. This is a useful and helpful tool and is by far the most generally useful type of meditation as opposed to contemplation or prayer.

The type of meditation which may be called visualization has as its goal not that which is contained in the meditation itself. Visualization is the tool of the adept. Those who learn to hold visual images in mind are developing an inner concentrative power that can transcend boredom and discomfort. When this ability has become crystallized in an adept the adept may then do polarizing in consciousness without external action which can affect the planetary consciousness. This is the reason for the existence of the so-called White Magician. Only those wishing to pursue the conscious raising of planetary vibration will find visualization to be a particularly satisfying type of meditation.

Contemplation or the consideration in a meditative state of an inspiring image or text is extremely useful also among your peoples, and the faculty of will, called praying is also of a potentially helpful nature. Whether it is indeed a helpful activity depends quite totally upon the intentions and objects of the one who prays."

Ra commended the (channeling) group (Don, Carla and Jim) for observing fatigue in the circle and refraining from a working until all were in love, harmony, and vital energy as one being. This is, and will continue to be, most helpful.

Session 50: 5-6-1981

Experiences are attracted into the entity through the south pole.

Ra: "I am Ra. It takes some consideration to accomplish the proper perspective for grasping the sense of the above information. The south or negative pole is one which attracts. It pulls unto itself those things magnetized to it. So, with the mind/body/spirit complex. The in-flow of experience is of the south pole influx. You may consider this a simplistic statement.

The only specific part of this correctness is that the red ray or foundation energy center, being the lowest or root energy center of the physical vehicle, will have the first opportunity to react to any experience. In this way only, you may see a physical locus (location) of the south pole being identified with the root energy center. In every facet of mind and body the root or foundation will be given the opportunity to function first.

What is this opportunity but survival? This is the root possibility of response and may be found to be characteristic of the basic functions of both mind and body. You will find this instinct the strongest, and once this is balanced much is open to the seeker. The south pole then ceases blocking the experiential data and higher energy centers of mind and body become availed of the opportunity to use the experience drawn to it."

Experiences are drawn to or attracted to the entity. Ra's understanding is that this is the nature of the phenomenon of experiential catalyst and its entry into the mind/body/spirit complex's awareness.

For example, this instrument, Carla Rueckert, chose, before incarnation, where catalyst can have a great probability of being obtained.

Ra: "This entity, Carla, desired the process of expressing love and light without expecting any return. This entity programmed also to endeavor (trying hard to accomplish) spiritual work and to comfort itself with companionship in the doing of work. (That's also what my channeling session revealed: That I'm supposed to teach spiritual topics such as channeling and the Law of One. I also wanted a relationship to help make life more enjoyable and easier. I believe the relationship helps keep me at a healthier level emotionally, so then I could complete even more spiritual work and service-to-others.)

Agreements were made prior to incarnation; first, with the so-called parents and siblings of this entity (of Carla). This provided the experiential catalyst for the situation of offering radiance of being without expectation of return. The second program involved agreements with several entities. These agreements provided and will provide, in your time/space and space/time continuum, opportunities for the experiential catalyst of work and comradeship.

There are events which were part of a program for this entity only in that they were possibility/probability vortices having to do with your societal culture. These events include the nature of the living or standard of living, the type of relationships entered into in your legal framework, and the social climate during incarnation. The incarnation was understood to be one which would take place at harvest.

These given, apply to millions of your peoples. Those aware of evolution and desirous in the very extreme of attaining the heart of love and the radiance which gives understanding no matter what the lessons programmed: they have to do with other selves, not with events: they have to do with giving, not receiving, for the lessons of love are of this nature both for positive and negative. Those negatively harvestable will be found at this time endeavoring to share their love of self.

There are those whose lessons are more random due to their present inability to comprehend the nature and mechanism of the evolution of mind, body, and spirit. Of these the process is guarded by those who never cease their watchful expectation of being of service. There is no entity without help, either through self-awareness of the unity of creation or through guardians of the self which protect the less sophisticated mind/body/spirit from any permanent separation from unity while the lessons of your density continue."

Ra may not use examples of known beings sharing love of self, due to the infringement that would cause. Therefore, Ra must be general. The negatively oriented being will be one who feels that it has found power that gives meaning to its existence. This negative entity will strive to offer these understandings to other selves, most usually by farming the elite, the disciples, and teaching the need and rightness of the enslavement of other selves for their own good. These other selves are conceived to be dependent upon the elite and in need of the guidance and the wisdom of the elite.

The adept is one who will go beyond the green ray that signals entry into harvestability. The adept will not simply be tapping into intelligent energy as a means of readiness for harvest but tapping into both intelligent energy and intelligent infinity for the purpose of transmuting planetary harvestability and consciousness.

The key is first, silence, and secondly, singleness of thought. Thusly, a visualization which can be held steady to the inward eye for several minutes. This will signal the adepts' increase in singleness of thought. This singleness of thought then can be used by the positive adept to work in group ritual visualizations for raising the positive energy. The negative adept visualizes for the increase in personal power.

When the positive adept touches intelligent infinity from within, this is the most powerful of connections for it is the connection of the whole mind/body/spirit complex microcosm (individual) with the macrocosm (universe). This connection enables the green-ray true color in time/space to manifest in our space/time. In green ray thoughts are beings. In our illusion this is not normally so.

The adepts then become living channels for love and light and are able to channel this radiance directly into the planetary web of energy nexi. The ritual will always end by the grounding of this energy in praise and thanksgiving and the release of this energy into the planetary whole.

The pyramid shape focuses the instreamings of energy for use by entities that may become aware of these instreamings. The shape of our physical brain is not significant for concentrating instreamings of energy.

Forgetting the pyramid will be of aid to the group in the study of the group feeling energy upon the head in meditation in various places.

Ra: "The instreamings of energy are felt by the energy centers which need activation and are prepared for, activation. Thus, those who feel the stimulation at violet-ray level are getting just that. Those feeling it within the forehead between the brows are experiencing indigo ray and so forth. Those experiencing tingling and visual images are having some blockage in the energy center being activated and thus the electrical body spreads this energy out and its effect is diffused (spread out).

Those not truly sincerely requesting this energy may yet feel it if the entities are not well trained in psychic defense. Those not desirous of experiencing these sensations and activations and changes even upon the subconscious level will not experience anything due to their abilities at defense and armoring against change."

The most normal for the adept is the indigo stimulation activating that great gateway into healing, magical work, prayerful attention, and the radiance of being; and the stimulation of violet ray which is the spiritual giving and taking from and to Creator, from Creator to Creator. This is a desirable configuration.

Why an entity must come into an incarnation and lose conscious memory of what he wants to do and then act in a way in which he hopes to act?

Ra answers: "Let us give the example of the man who sees all the poker hands. He then knows the game. It is but child's play to gamble, for it is no risk. The other hands are known. The possibilities are known and the hand will be played correctly but with no interest.

In time/space (invisible space) and in the true color green density (4th density), the hands of all are open to the eye. The thoughts, the feelings, the troubles, all these may be seen. There

100

is no deception and no desire for deception. Thus, much may be accomplished in harmony but the mind/body/spirit gains little polarity from this interaction.

Let us re-examine this metaphor and multiply it into the longest poker game you can imagine, a lifetime. The cards are love, dislike, limitation, unhappiness, pleasure, etc. They are dealt and re-dealt and re-dealt continuously. You may, during this incarnation begin and we stress begin- to know your own cards. You may begin to find the love within you. You may begin to balance your pleasure, your limitations, etc. However, your only indication of other selves' cards is to look into the eyes.

You cannot remember your hand, their hands, perhaps even the rules of this game. This game can only be won by those who lose their cards in the melting influence of love, can only be won by those who lay their pleasures, their limitations, their all upon the table face up and say inwardly: "All, all of you players, each other self, whatever your hand, I love you." This is the game: to know, to accept, to forgive, to balance, and to open the self in love. This cannot be done without the forgetting, for it would carry no weight in the life of the mind/body/spirit beingness totality."

END of BOOK 2 of 5

<u>Keep in Touch:</u>

STAY IN TOUCH! Add me, and let's be friends, or just follow to get free information that will rapidly change your life for the better.

<u>~Email:</u> authorkathrynjordyn@gmail.com

<u>YouTube channel:</u> http://youtube.com/@Kathryn_Jordyn

(This channel will talk about BMX, personal things, inspirational things, wisdom, thoughts, knowledge, and metaphysical concepts on spirituality.) (I'm also going to be talking about Metaphysics, the Law of One, and the Truth about the Bible that no one talks about.)

Instagram= @AuthorKathrynJordyn

TikTok= @kathrynjordyn

Facebook= Kathryn Jordyn

YouTube= http://youtube.com/@Kathryn_Jordyn

Join for free: Patreon= patreon.com/AuthorKathrynJordyn

~ I found my soulmate and started to manifest after I put my all into serving others after making sure my own needs were met first, as we both are around 87-90% positively-oriented service-to-others. ~

*Come along for the Ride, for future projects and videos.

Shop for Charity:

http://author-kathryn-jordyn.printify.me/